INSTRUCTIONAL LEADERSHIP

*A publication of the Horace Mann-Lincoln
Institute of School Experimentation
Teachers College, Columbia University*

INSTRUCTIONAL LEADERSHIP

by Gordon N. Mackenzie and Stephen M. Corey

HORACE MANN-LINCOLN INSTITUTE
OF SCHOOL EXPERIMENTATION
TEACHERS COLLEGE, COLUMBIA UNIVERSITY

in association with
James Hall, Veronica Casey, Mary Neel Smith, and others

BUREAU OF PUBLICATIONS

Teachers College   Columbia University   New York   1954

FOREWORD

Administrative and supervisory officers generally are concerned with improving the work of teachers. Rarely do they give serious attention to improving their own competence as instructional leaders. The present report is refreshing and encouraging, for it shows what those with official leadership positions can do if they study their own jobs. The attitude toward leadership responsibility demonstrated by the participants in this study is one which it is to be hoped will become much more common in American schools than it now is. Improved instructional leadership is a sure road to improved instruction.

The study has three features that should make it especially useful for supervisory and administrative officers. First, it presents a carefully reasoned conception of the nature of instructional leadership. This should assist all persons who have official leadership responsibilities in education to appraise critically their own views of their jobs. Second, it demonstrates how a group of school leaders can test more objectively than is customary the success of their efforts and modify their plans in the light of the evidence they obtain. Third, it gives some indication of the effectiveness of various activities in improving instructional leadership.

This is a pioneering study in an important respect. The Denver leadership project is the first project known to the writer in which a group of instructional leaders joined together over an extended period of time to study intensively and critically the jobs they were doing. One gets the impression that the participants gained far more than can be shown in a written report. Perhaps the most important implication of the study is that great values may be realized by those who will take the time and trouble to turn the light of research on their own activities.

HOLLIS L. CASWELL

PREFACE

This volume is the report of three years of cooperative study undertaken to improve instructional leadership.
The people directly involved were members of the Denver,
Colorado, public school instructional staff and two consultants from the Horace Mann-Lincoln Institute of School Experimentation of Teachers College, Columbia University.
The Denver participants included the principals of all the
junior and senior high schools, a coordinator of instruction
from each of these schools, and several representatives from
the central office of the Department of Instruction.

From 1949 to 1952, while the study was being carried on,
many different activities were undertaken. (1) Each of
twelve two- or three-day meetings of the total group was
attended by thirty-five to forty people. (2) Many individuals engaged in such subgroup projects as identifying desirable leadership beliefs and practices, improving methods
of interpreting research data, and studying school-commu-
nity relations. (3) The principal and coordinator from each
school worked as a team on a specific project of their choice,
in consultation with the Horace Mann-Lincoln Institute consultants. (4) Several continuing committees worked for vary-

ing periods of time. (5) At the beginning of the project and for several months thereafter, the total group was divided into three subgroups, each concerned with a specific problem area. (6) A five-day workshop was held in June, 1950. (7) Many of the participants engaged in a great deal of reading and discussion about leadership. (8) Between visits of the consultants to Denver there was frequent written correspondence between them and the Denver participants. All these activities are described in greater detail in Chapter 6.

The method we tried to use in improving our leadership practices was a kind of action research, and attempts were made to obtain as much evidence as possible concerning results. In October, 1951, two days were devoted to a rather formal evaluation of the project. Most of the year 1952 was devoted to the cooperative writing of this book.

The participants in the leadership project considered at some length the most useful organization for the written report of activities and findings. It was decided to divide the book into two parts. Part I elaborates the conception of instructional leadership that proved most helpful to us, evaluates different ways of exercising leadership, discusses situational factors that seemed to influence the kind of instructional leadership we wanted to exercise, and describes methods of improving leadership. Although the argument of Part I is not supported at all points by concrete evidence derived from the Denver project, it does represent our major conclusions and is illustrated copiously from our experiences.

Part II includes those chapters in which the Denver setting and the activities we engaged in are described and the general chronology of events, some of the more general learnings, and a few of the findings resulting from our experimentation with leadership in small working groups are reported. This second section is concluded by a chapter in which an analysis of the evaluation data obtained during the meeting in October, 1951, is presented. The data were analyzed separately by the Denver group and the Institute consultants. Later the two groups met and combined their interpretations.

The general discussion of leadership is presented first because we think it will be of interest to all readers concerned about instructional leadership. The Denver studies deal with a number of specific instructional problems, and the report of them will, we believe, be of value to those who are trying to cope with similar problems.

The ideas in this book could not have been developed cooperatively, as they were, without the psychological and material support of Kenneth Oberholzer, superintendent of the Denver school system, and Roy Hinderman, deputy superintendent. These men expressed in words and deeds their interest in our efforts to develop better ideas about instructional leadership and to test some of these in practice. The policy of the Denver schools has, for many years, placed great emphasis on in-service education, and the leadership project was greatly furthered because of this emphasis.

Many of the Denver participants were involved in the actual writing of this report. James Hall, formerly director of secondary school instruction in Denver and now superintendent of schools in Port Washington, New York, prepared initial drafts of Chapters 5 and 6. Mary Neel Smith and Veronica Casey did the same for Chapter 7. The final draft of the entire manuscript was read critically by Mr. Hall, Mrs. Smith, and Miss Casey, as well as by Mary Lee Keath, Lucille Darrah, Roy Hinderman, and Ruth Wagner —all of the Denver public schools. Numerous improvements were made as a result of their criticisms. Several members of the staff of the Horace Mann-Lincoln Institute of School Experimentation maintained a continued interest in the project. Dean Hollis L. Caswell of Teachers College read a late draft of the manuscript and suggested several changes.

If we were asked what we consider to be the major purpose of this report of three years of study, our answer would be that we hope our experience, which was valuable to us, will stimulate other instructional leaders in other school systems to engage in a similar study of their activities. If the elaboration of the generalizations we arrived at and the discussion of our successes and failures are of help to them, we shall be amply rewarded.

GORDON N. MACKENZIE
STEPHEN M. COREY
Horace Mann-Lincoln Institute
of School Experimentation

CONTENTS

FOREWORD *Hollis L. Caswell*   v

PREFACE   vii

Part One THE NATURE AND IMPROVEMENT
            OF INSTRUCTIONAL LEADERSHIP

1 OUR CONCEPTION OF LEADERSHIP   3
  The Meaning of Leadership   4
  Four Components of Leadership Situations   10
  Effect of Leadership-Situation Components on
      Leadership and Selection of Leaders   14
  Points Not Covered in This Chapter   18

2 WAYS OF EXERCISING LEADERSHIP IN SCHOOL SITUATIONS   21
  Instructional Responsibility of Principals and
      Curriculum Coordinators   22
  Four Ways of Exercising Leadership   23
  Factors Influencing Status Leader's Selection of
      Leadership Method   31
  Superiority of Mutual Goals-Means Leadership   33
  Status Leader's Role in Mutual Goals-Means
      Leadership   35
  Summary   41

3 PEOPLE AS SITUATIONAL FACTORS AFFECTING LEADER-
SHIP   43
   Individual Differences   43
   Interpersonal Relations   56
   School Organization   68

4 IMPROVEMENT OF INSTRUCTIONAL LEADERSHIP   74
   Conditions Essential to an Effective Leadership
     Education Program   76
   The Leadership Learning Process   82
   Learning Experiences Contributing to Leader-
     ship Improvement   96

Part Two THE DENVER LEADERSHIP PROJECT

5 THE DENVER SETTING   103
   Denver Curriculum Improvement Policy   105
   The Leadership Project   106

6 PROJECT ACTIVITIES   111
   The Total Group   111
   The Subgroups   118
   The Workshop   123
   The Building Teams   124
   The Consultants   135

7 LEADERSHIP IN SMALL FACE-TO-FACE GROUPS   137
   Committee Formation   139
   Task Identification   145
   Meetings: Physical Arrangements, Time Allot-
     ment, Opportunities for Acquaintance 151
   Methods of Improving Communication   156
   Methods of Increasing Participation   159
   Forms and Records   163
   Obstacles to Effective Group Work   166

8 AN EVALUATION OF THE LEADERSHIP PROJECT   168
   Group Expectations   168

CONTENTS

Learning Activities 173
General Achievements 174
Changes in Leadership Practices 179
Changes in Leadership Concepts and Beliefs 187
Our Mistakes 193
Summary 197

APPENDIX
Denver Leadership Project Publications 201
"Ideas about Myself" Inventory 202

INDEX 205

Part One THE NATURE AND IMPROVEMENT
OF INSTRUCTIONAL LEADERSHIP

1

OUR CONCEPTION OF LEADERSHIP

Much that has been written about leadership is difficult to interpret and use because the authors give no indication of what they mean by *leadership*. In order to communicate with one another and establish a clear reference point for our work and study, we found it necessary to clarify the meaning of the term *leadership*. The definition we developed appeared to us to apply to all kinds of leadership, "good" and "bad." It is an attempt to describe the nature of leadership under all conditions.

For purposes of discussion and analysis, we found it helpful to separate the leadership process, or what the leader does, from the characteristics of the leader himself and from the various roles that may be associated with leadership positions. A status, or official, leader[1]—a principal, curriculum coordinator, or superintendent—has many roles and responsibilities, only some of which involve working with other people. Activities such as clerical work, creative writing, editorial work, management of personal time schedules, and

---

[1] The terms *status leader* and *official leader* are used to refer to persons holding such official positions as superintendent, principal, assistant principal, curriculum coordinator—persons assumed to have official responsibility for instructional leadership.

3

administrative routines entail responsibilities that do not usually necessitate leadership. They are individually performed activities in which others are not ordinarily involved. Status leaders may display a wide range of traits or characteristics, all of which influence their success but only some of which relate to leadership roles.

In Chapter 2 we expand our definition of *leadership* and consider what we believe to be "good" leadership—leadership adequate for a program of instructional improvement in a democracy. In that chapter we also explore the implications of this definition for status leaders in education. In later chapters we describe the process by which the definition was developed and discuss some of the values we believe resulted from our efforts to clarify our ideas about leadership.

The Meaning of Leadership

Our conception of leadership can probably best be understood if leadership is viewed as a natural accompaniment of the goal-seeking behavior of human beings. From birth until death, people appear to be either restlessly seeking things or conditions they believe will be better than the things they possess or the conditions that exist or striving to maintain what they believe to be good. They may want to acquire greater skill in human relations, or increased physical strength, or more cunning, or additional money. Sometimes they may want only to maintain the status quo; in that case they may be relatively inactive unless they believe existing arrangements to be threatened. Goal-seeking behavior characterizes all human beings, regardless of whether they know exactly what they are seeking or what will satisfy them most.

In the process of seeking to maintain the status quo, to achieve something desired, or to find satisfactions only dimly perceived or possibly not perceived at all, help is frequently needed and received. The key to our conception of leadership lies in an understanding of the process of giving and receiving help in order to maintain an existing condition against threat, to identify new goals, or to attain goals that are known and defined. Assistance in accomplishing any one of these tasks, or a combination of all of them, may be sought by individuals or groups in order to increase their satisfactions.

Assistance in Identifying a Goal

The following illustration may clarify the process involved in the identification or establishment of a goal as well as the kind of assistance leading to its establishment. Teacher A had taught social studies in the same school for many years. She was a systematic individual with a well-organized routine, which permitted her to teach her classes with a minimum of daily preparation. Students liked her, but they as well as her colleagues recognized that she did the same things in her classes year after year. After hearing her students discuss enthusiastically the planning they were doing with Teacher B, Teacher A decided to find out what Teacher B was doing. She became intensely interested and decided to try the process in her class. For several years she has been experimenting with student participation in planning. She has constantly improved her methods and procedures. Recently she has started writing for professional journals and talking at educational conferences about what she is doing.

It seems safe to assume that Teacher B, or possibly the students through their enthusiastic discussion of planning in Teacher B's class, so aroused Teacher A's interest in teacher-student planning that it became a focal point for much of her activity. Involving students in planning for social studies classes became a goal to which she devoted intensive attention.

The people who stimulated Teacher A can be viewed as helping her to identify or establish a goal that proved to be

5

satisfying. Teacher A frequently gives credit to Teacher B for arousing her interest in student participation in planning. She also gives credit publicly to Teacher B for helping her learn the skills necessary for directing this participation.

We have, then, an illustration of one person, Teacher B, helping another person, Teacher A, (1) to establish a goal —involving students in planning—and (2) to move toward that goal by learning the skills necessary for directing student participation in planning. Furthermore, Teacher A recognized clearly that Teacher B had helped her (1) to develop an interest in student participation in planning and (2) to learn the skills necessary for facilitating this participation.

It is quite possible that Teacher A received kinds of assistance other than those she recognized. The enthusiasm of the students for Teacher B's class may have helped to arouse Teacher A's interest. There is also the possibility that after Teacher A had decided to try student participation in planning in her own classes, she received help from magazine articles, lectures, and other teachers, although she may not have recognized or been aware of these other sources of help.

Any of the activities of others that helped Teacher A identify or achieve her goal can be cited as instances of leadership. Those who performed the activities that were of help can be referred to as leaders. However, only Teacher B is *recognized* as a leader by Teacher A. The activities of Teacher B considered helpful by Teacher A therefore constitute *recognized* leadership.

Assistance in Achieving a Goal

It may be helpful to turn to another illustration, one in which a goal as well as possible means of achieving the goal were clearly recognized. A curriculum coordinator wanted to improve the interpersonal relations of staff members with

6

whom he worked. He saw the following as possible means of attaining this goal: (1) serving coffee before staff meetings; (2) planning a week-end conference on instructional problems at a resort in the mountains; (3) improving or discontinuing a rating procedure; and (4) minimizing the influence of status factors at group meetings. He wanted to try all of these in order to achieve his goal of better human relations.

The coordinator realized that he did not have very complete control over what needed to be done to achieve his purpose. He therefore turned to others for help. He asked the principal for assistance in obtaining school funds to pay for the coffee to be served before staff meetings. He asked the chairman of the curriculum council for help in arranging the week-end conference on instructional problems. Those activities of the principal and the chairman of the curriculum council that are recognized by the coordinator as helping him to attain his desired goal constitute recognized leadership. The coordinator turned for help to the people who, in his opinion, possessed the understanding, skills, or material means he considered necessary for achieving his goal. These people he thought of, or recognized, as leaders. Generalizing from this illustration, it can be said that if one or more persons perceive an individual as helping them or being able to help them establish purposes or achieve known purposes, this individual becomes, for them, a recognized leader.

It is quite possible, however, that in the illustration just given there were also some instances of unrecognized leadership. The curriculum coordinator may have heard a lecturer discuss a week-end conference as one method of improving human relations. He may have come to see the values of a week-end conference and learned many things about conducting one as a result of taking part in such a conference while employed in another school system. Both the lecturer and the sponsors of the week-end conference in which the coordinator participated may have helped him to

7

achieve his goal, but the coordinator may not have recognized his indebtedness to these sources of assistance.

Let us assume that when the curriculum coordinator went to the chairman of the curriculum council for help in arranging the conference, the chairman took a questioning attitude, raised objections, and pointed out problems and difficulties. These activities might be regarded by the coordinator as blocking his efforts. But if the chairman, by his questioning, caused the coordinator to think more carefully about the proposed conference and to formulate plans that would meet possible objections, the chairman would have been helping the coordinator to achieve his goal even if the coordinator did not recognize the help he was receiving. In other words, we might think of the chairman as also providing leadership that was not recognized.

If the chairman had refused help in arranging the conference but had offered to give a lecture on human relations instead, he would have been suggesting an alternative means. Although theoretically the lecture might have helped to improve human relations, the chairman would not have been displaying leadership, as far as the coordinator was concerned, unless the coordinator recognized the lecture as a means he wanted used or as an effective method of improving human relations. Thus, the key to recognized leadership is the ability and willingness to provide means that individuals or groups either desire to use or accept as useful in defining new goals or attaining known and defined goals. The means may be materials, a particular skill, the authority needed to go ahead, or any other form of assistance. This ability to provide means acceptable to or desired by individuals or groups we shall refer to as *control of means*.

There are situations in which several individuals may have control of means other individuals or groups desire to use. In such situations a choice may be made in favor of the person believed to have greatest control and thus believed to be able to provide the most help.

8

Leadership may be exercised by anyone who is seen as having some control of means others desire to use. The implications of this will be considered more fully in later chapters. Here, however, it should be emphasized that we believe it is helpful (1) not to equate leadership with any appointive, elective, or hereditary position and (2) to recognize that every individual probably has control of some means someone else wants to use and is able to a certain extent, through study and practice, to increase this control. This statement implies, of course, that most individuals can improve their leadership. The holding of an official leadership position is not necessary for the control of means.

The idea that every individual can be a leader suggests that a number of actual and potential leaders may simultaneously be members of a group endeavoring to identify or establish goals, decide on means of attaining identified goals, or maintain a situation against threat. The leader may be anyone who is recognized by individuals or by the group as an available source of help in deciding what to do or how to do it. Any suggestions accepted as helpful by others indicate leadership on the part of those presenting the suggestions. They are the manifestation, in action, of the ability to provide means others desire to use in identifying or achieving their goals.

After thinking about many illustrations of what we considered to be leadership, we finally stated our definition of *recognized leader* and *recognized leadership* as follows:[2]

[2] The following sources, particularly the articles by Knickerbocker and McGregor, were of help to us in developing this definition and some of its implications:

Alvin W. Gouldner, *Studies in Leadership* (New York, Harper and Brothers, 1950).

Irving R. Knickerbocker, "Leadership: A Conception and Some Implications," *Journal of Social Issues*, 4:23–40, Summer 1948.

David Krech and Richard S. Crutchfield, *Theory and Problems of Social Psychology* (New York, McGraw-Hill Book Company, Inc., 1948).

Douglas McGregor, "The Staff Function in Human Relations," *Journal of Social Issues*, 4:5–22, Summer 1948.

A *"recognized leader"* is a person who is seen by individuals or groups as helping or being able to help provide the means they desire to use to identify or attain their goals.

"Recognized leadership" is a name for those activities that are seen by individuals or groups as helping or potentially helping to provide the means they desire to use to identify or attain their goals.

Having arrived at these two definitions, we still faced many problems and questions. We realized that the definitions, if strictly applied, might mean that the group, in certain situations, was leading an individual. This sometimes happens. We were aware that many implications of the definitions needed exploration and clarification. In this process we found it helpful to give primary attention to leadership rather than the leader. The *activities* of the leader seemed to be the key to the relationship between leaders and followers. Furthermore, while we realized we might not be able to change our personalities, we felt that we would be able to analyze and modify our activities and behavior to a certain extent.

Four Components of Leadership Situations

As we continued to examine the definition of *leadership* and the activities that might be helpful to others in identifying or attaining their goals, we recognized that these activities, and hence leadership, varied with situations. Leadership is not something fixed or static. The activities that constitute leadership are largely determined by the situation in which leadership is exercised, and the situations in which leaders function are diverse and complex. Our analysis of these situations revealed at least four variables, each of which determines, in part, what individuals or groups will find helpful.

10

The Goals Sought

The goals individuals or groups seek may vary from time to time and from individual to individual or group to group. A particular group may be striving to reach consensus at one time and trying to engage in community singing at another. One group may be striving to reach consensus and a different group may be engaged in community singing. Thus, the goals one group seeks may differ from those sought by another group. There are, of course, analogous differences in goals among individuals.

It is clear that the activities necessary for helping a group reach consensus, for example, would not be the same as those that would make community singing possible. Consequently, the person able to be of greatest help to a group trying to achieve consensus might be of no help at all to a group engaged in community singing. The person recognized as a leader in one situation might not be a leader in another.

This specificity of leadership qualifications deserves emphasis. It is common to put a halo around the head of the person who provides help in achieving certain major goals and to assume that this individual can provide effective leadership in general. Actually, the range of leadership activities at the command of one individual is usually limited. Clear identification of both the specific goals to be sought and the means to be employed in achieving these goals may suggest the qualifications needed by the individual who will be able to provide the most help.

The Means Desired

The means individuals or groups perceive as helpful in identifying a goal or desire to use in attaining a particular goal vary from situation to situation. It is not unusual to find staff members who have not previously worked together as a group struggling to decide whether or not they should co-

11

operatively study some school problem. They are trying to discover whether or not a goal that challenges them sufficiently can be identified and whether or not there is any value in working cooperatively toward the achievement of this goal. The help some individuals give one group in deciding whether a problem or goal is worthy of its effort and attention may not help another group in identifying its goal. The activities that help a group at one time may not be helpful on another occasion.

Perhaps the problem is one of achieving rather than identifying a goal. A staff trying to reach consensus regarding the desirability of a two- or three-year period of cooperative, intensive study of students by the total staff group might try to achieve this goal in several ways. One might involve three meetings of the staff, spread over a period of one month during the spring prior to the initiation of the study and devoted to a consideration of possible values, methods of working, and the interests of individual staff members. Another way of achieving the same goal—consensus—might involve ten minutes of consideration in which participants are urged to reach a decision quickly because it is necessary to complete arrangements with a consultant before the next meeting of the board of education.

These two different ways of achieving the same goal might be used by one group at two different times or by two different groups. The activities of the leaders, however, would be quite different. The person who can provide leadership in a protracted deliberative situation may become panicky when a quick decision is required. Thus, the individual who has a substantial degree of control of means in one situation may not have this control in another.

The Control of Means by Actual and Potential Leaders

The means controlled by an individual may vary from time to time and from situation to situation. A person who

12

may be able to help one group achieve its goals may be unable to assist another. He may be able to help a group at one time without being able to do so on another occasion. A curriculum coordinator may have the verbal facility, under-standing, and skills that cause a group of general education teachers to regard him as very helpful, and therefore as pro-viding effective leadership, in their efforts to modify their instruction to meet student needs. The same curriculum coordinator may not have the verbal facility, understanding, and skills that would cause a group of vocational teachers to regard him as helpful, and therefore as providing effective leadership, in their efforts to modify their instruction to meet student needs. It is quite possible to note similar variations from one time to another. The curriculum coordinator who was recognized by the general education teachers as a leader in 1945 might not be so recognized in 1955. Variations in the control of means by the same individual in different situa-tions may be due (1) to variations in the potential leader himself under varying conditions or (2) to variations in the perceptions of the individuals or groups with whom he is working.

At any specific time there may or may not be potential leaders available who control means that will be of help to an individual or a group. A teacher may desire help in using sociograms effectively but may not be able to locate an in-dividual from whom he can secure the needed assistance. He might, therefore, postpone his use of sociograms, or experi-ment with sociograms on his own, or search for assistance in the professional literature. Similarly, a group of teachers may desire to appeal to a legislative body for assistance on pensions but may not have a representative in whom it has confidence. It might therefore postpone action. The num-ber or quality of potential leaders available often determines what individuals or groups try to do as well as how they seek to arrive at their goals.

13

The Physical Conditions and Psychological Climate

Variations in psychological climate and physical conditions may influence the perceptions and activities of individuals and groups, leaders and potential leaders. This component of leadership situations may in part explain some of the variations in goals sought, in means desired, and in control of means by potential leaders. Thus, a group in the habit of trying to resolve problems on the basis of consensus might, at the end of a long meeting, when many of the members were exhausted, resort to a hasty decision by majority vote. The psychological climate would be in part a consequence of fatigue, and would influence the group's method of making a decision.

The same group, after what to its members had been an unsatisfactory series of staff meetings, might, in an effort to improve meetings, engage in a long and careful study of a staff member's proposal that all meetings be held in the morning before school. However, a sudden announcement from the central office, proposing that all staff meetings be held on Tuesday afternoons for the next year, might result in a hurried, poorly planned meeting in which an effort is made to arrive at consensus and respond to the proposal. And, as we have said earlier, the person who is skillful in guiding the group during the slow, drawn-out deliberation might literally go to pieces in a hastily planned session.

Effect of Leadership-Situation Components on Leadership and Selection of Leaders

As has already been suggested, the way in which the components of leadership situations are interrelated determines what kind of leaders will be selected as well as the activities in which the leader will engage. The four components identified in the preceding section are (1) the goals

14

individuals or groups are seeking; (2) the means individuals or groups perceive as helpful in the identification of goals or desire to use in the achievement of known goals; (3) the goals, motivations, understandings, and skills of potential and actual leaders in any given situation; and (4) the physical conditions and psychological climate in which the group functions.

An illustration may help to clarify how the selection of leaders and the activities constituting leadership are affected by these factors. Let us assume a situation in which a school staff has developed a core program for grades seven and eight. After the program has been in effect for two years, and in spite of efforts to inform the parents of its merit, there is evidence of mounting parental dissatisfaction. The criticisms made by the mothers and fathers include the following: the core program will not prepare children adequately for college; the students are no longer learning grammar; the program is merely a fad, is experimental, and should be tested somewhere else before being put into effect here; the students waste a lot of time planning—teachers ought to know what students should learn.

The staff members meet to consider this situation. They reaffirm their conviction that the core program represents sound educational policy. They believe, furthermore, that it can be improved. Yet the criticism of the parents is such that the teachers believe something should be done to meet it. A proposal that the staff discuss specific actions that might be taken in order to influence the attitude of the parents is accepted.

Among the numerous suggestions made, four stand out as representing distinct differences in methods the group might use to save the core program. Each of these methods has several advocates, and each may be viewed as suggesting different activities in which the person chosen as leader will engage.

15

One teacher proposes that the group agree to stand firm and do what it can to *force* acceptance of the core. "If we are able to announce that we have considered the various criticisms and are unanimous in our decision that the core represents sound educational policy and should be continued, I believe we can force the public to recognize its merits. We shouldn't let the critics discourage us or make us give up this good program. As a professional group, we know what is best educationally. There is no reason why we should permit uninformed parents to interfere."

Another teacher proposes that the program be saved by compromising, or *bargaining*. "Let's recognize some of these criticisms and meet the parents halfway. Let's teach a little more grammar, reduce the amount of student participation and planning, and develop a fairly complete course of study for the core program. If we do these things, I think the parents will meet us halfway and accept most of the core."

Another teacher proposes that the staff tell the public about the tremendous amount of effort and care that has gone into planning the core program in order to give their children a better education. "Why not tell the parents of the time and energy we've put in developing this core in order to give their children a better education? We spent a whole year studying core programs before we ever started. We visited other school systems. We brought in outside consultants. We've spent afternoons and evenings planning our program. A group of us put in a summer at the university. All of us who teach in this program spend much more time planning now than we did before. We take more trips with students and devote more time to their out-of-school activities. I think if the parents really knew what we've done and are doing for their children, they would appreciate our efforts and accept the program." This proposal can be viewed as a special type of bargaining, one with *paternalistic* implications. It stresses the importance of impressing parents

16

with the good intentions and actions of teachers and counts on them to show their gratitude by accepting the teachers' proposals.

A fourth teacher suggests that the staff work harder for *mutual understanding* on the part of teachers and lay citizens. "We've done a lot of work developing this core. We have convinced ourselves but not the parents. Probably we don't understand their feelings well enough, and maybe they don't understand ours. I suggest that we invite all interested parents, and especially those who are critical, to participate in a series of six or ten meetings in which we can study the views of teachers and parents, look at some of the evidence of the worth of the core, and then decide as a total group what should be done. We might well bring students in, too, so that all the people who have a stake in this program can work together for a mutually satisfactory understanding of what we are trying to do and how it should be done."

Although all the teachers agree on the goal—maintaining the core program—each of the four subgroups regards a different way of achieving the goal as most appropriate. Those in subgroup one might select as a leader a person they believe will be able to help them maintain the core program by *forcing* the public to accept it. Those in subgroup two might select a person they view as being able to help them maintain the core program by *bargaining,* or compromising, with the parents. Those in subgroup three might select still another leader, one they believe will be able to help them maintain the core by publicizing the careful study that preceded the program and the amount of time and energy the staff has voluntarily given and is continuing to give to it. We called this a *paternalistic* approach. Those in subgroup four might select still a fourth person, one they consider able to help them maintain the core by creating a *mutual understanding* of goals and means relative to the program.

Each of the subgroups selects a different method of achiev-

17

ing the common goal. Each group might select a different kind of leader, one who can best assist with the method it wants to use. Despite agreement on the goal, therefore, disagreement on approaches might result in controversy and friction within the total group. Quite often, individuals and groups have a limited understanding of the relative merit of a variety of methods by which their aims can be achieved. As a result, they frequently change their leaders when new methods become apparent, or when new evidence is introduced in support of methods that were formerly rejected.

The influence of psychological climate on the selection of leaders and the activities constituting leadership can be illustrated by an extension of the example given in the preceding paragraphs. If the community is one in which public sentiment is strongly opposed to any group's resorting to force in order to maintain a particular school program, and if the teachers are or become aware of this feeling, they will probably regard it as one important argument against the use of force. Such a consideration might cause the group to concentrate on bargaining, paternalism, attempts to reach mutual understanding, or a combination of two or more of these.

Points Not Covered in This Chapter

Defining *leadership* as we have and calling attention to situational variables that influence the selection of leaders and the activities that constitute leadership seemed to us to provide a satisfactory basis for developing a useful theory of leadership. Several problems suggested by the definition, however, have not been dealt with in this chapter.

First, the definition may appear to be inconsistent with other conceptions of leadership. There is a rather common expectation in our culture that the school principal, for example, should make decisions for his staff and then see

18

that the decisions are carried out. This expectation is shared by many lay citizens, school board members, and even central office personnel.

Second, no clear relation has been established between the definition presented here and some of the adjectives commonly used today to characterize leadership—adjectives such as *autocratic, democratic,* or *laissez-faire.*

Third, no clear relation has been established between the definition as stated and the role of the status, or official, leader—the person to whom a leadership role is assigned by someone outside a particular staff group. The illustrations used in this chapter have emphasized situations in which individuals or groups seeking to accomplish some goal recognize that a particular individual has control of means necessary for achieving this goal and either elect him to a leadership position or spontaneously accept his leadership. The status leader faces the problem of serving as a leader, not only for his staff, but for students and the lay public as well. He may also have a leadership responsibility toward central office personnel and the board of education. The idea that a leadership role can be assigned to a principal, for example, by anyone other than his staff group, which perceives him to have control of means it wishes to use to attain its goals, clearly presents some problems.

A fourth point that has not been discussed is the rather widespread belief in leadership traits. The definition we have accepted and presented stresses situational influences. No mention has been made of inherited or developed traits as factors in leadership. Yet much of the literature on leadership assumes or emphasizes that the presence or absence of certain traits determines the presence or absence of leadership.

A fifth omission concerns the evaluation of leadership. The discussion in this chapter might justify the inference that the sole criterion for judging the quality of leadership

19

is the extent to which individuals or groups believe they are getting help in the achievement of their goals. Yet it is reasonable to assume that some goals sought by individuals or groups are better than other goals. Also, it seems reasonable to suppose that some means of achieving a particular goal may be much better or much worse than others.

Some of these points will be considered in the next two chapters.

2

WAYS OF EXERCISING LEADERSHIP IN SCHOOL SITUATIONS

In Chapter 1 *recognized leadership* was defined as "a name for those activities that are seen by individuals or groups as helping or potentially helping to provide the means they desire to use to identify or attain their goals." This definition appeared to us to apply to all kinds of leadership under all conditions. However, it did not enable us to judge the quality of leadership. We were sure that some ways of exercising leadership are better than other ways and eventually developed criteria for assessing leadership quality. The criteria are based on the assumption that that leadership is best which results in the greatest good for the greatest number of people. This assumption calls attention to the importance of involving in the problem solving process, whenever possible and to the degree possible, all persons who will be affected by any action that is taken.

The criteria we developed are three in number. First, good leadership meets the needs and preferences of group members. Second, good leadership utilizes what is known about human motivation by relating activity and its conse-

21

quences so that the efforts of members of a working group are intrinsically rather than extrinsically motivated. Third, good leadership elicits the maximum contribution of each member of the problem solving group. This requires a wise use of human resources and is in accordance with the democratic belief in the worth of each individual.

In this chapter, after discussing the leadership responsibilities of principals and curriculum coordinators, we compare four methods of exercising leadership—force, bargaining, paternalism, and cooperative determination of mutually acceptable goals and means. We comment on the influence of situational factors on the leadership methods used by status leaders and consider briefly the superiority of mutual goals-means leadership on the basis of the three criteria just stated. The chapter is concluded with a discussion of the role of the status leader in fostering the cooperative determination of goals and means of achieving these goals.

As noted earlier, the Denver project was focused on the instructional leadership of secondary school principals and curriculum coordinators. Our consideration of leadership quality is therefore presented in the context of instructional leadership at the individual school level.

Instructional Responsibility of Principals and Curriculum Coordinators

Status leaders in charge of instruction in an individual school are, in a broad sense, responsible for mobilizing the abilities and efforts of the teaching staff to provide an effective educational program. In general, this means that they are expected to develop a favorable climate for staff work and to coordinate the efforts of various staff members. Individual status leaders—principals, assistant principals, or curriculum coordinators—may be assigned specific responsibilities within this broad area.

Four Ways of Exercising Leadership

As has been stated, most of the illustrations in Chapter 1 dealt with situations in which leaders were selected or accepted by individuals or groups because they controlled means viewed as useful by these individuals or groups. In this chapter we consider leaders who are selected in another way—leaders who are appointed to their position by someone outside the group in which they will function. The appointing agency usually endeavors to select a person who will be able to provide help to his group because he possesses certain values, understandings, and skills. The appointing agency also endeavors to give the appointee control of certain other means—property, money, authority—that will increase his leadership potential.

When a leader is appointed, his activities may be viewed as contributing to the achievement of his own goals or to the achievement of the goals of those who appoint him. However, there can be no leadership, in respect to the group he is appointed to lead, unless the members of the group recognize him as controlling means *they* desire to use to identify or achieve *their* goals. This means that one of the following conditions must obtain: (1) the leader's goals must be those of the group, and he must be seen by the group as helping or potentially helping it to achieve its goals; (2) the leader's goals must be sufficiently compatible with those of the group so that the group sees him as helping or potentially helping it to achieve its goals; (3) the group must recognize the leader as helping to avoid destruction of a desired status quo or as offering the least threat to its goal achievement; (4) the goals toward which the leader is viewed by the group as being able to contribute essential help must be important enough to offset or outweigh his refusal or inability to help the group achieve some of its other goals.

23

In Chapter 1, (1) force, (2) bargaining, (3) paternalism, and (4) determination of mutually acceptable goals and means were described as different methods by which a group might attempt to influence the attitude and activities of parents. In this section the selection among the same four ways of working is looked at from the point of view of the status leader. He too will have predilections and convictions about his role, and these, together with certain situational factors, will influence his choice of leadership method. As we have said, status leaders in charge of instruction at the building level have this major assigned responsibility: to mobilize the abilities and efforts of the teaching staff for an effective instructional program.

Force

Status leaders may, through control of scarce or vitally important means, force teachers to engage in activities not viewed by them as contributing to the achievement of their personal or professional goals. The activities they are forced to engage in are considered by the teachers to be only less undesirable than what might happen if the status leader exercised his power to withhold means they consider essential to their achievement of other important goals. The method of force is possible when teachers find it difficult to secure another position or, for one reason or another, do not wish to or cannot leave the position they hold.

A status leader may decide that in order to improve instruction, each teacher should read a book dealing with curriculum problems and report on it to the staff. He announces his plan, selects the books, and assigns them to individual teachers, designating the dates on which each is to report. This may all be done with enthusiasm and in a pleasant and straightforward manner. There is no open show of force, but it is being exercised nevertheless. The teachers are skeptical of the value of the assigned reading and reporting. A few are violently opposed. Some become very anxious at the thought of going before their peers to report. In the teachers' room, criticisms of the plan increase as each successive report is given. Some of the teachers still on probation think it unwise to let the status leader know of their objections. They fear that the annual evaluation he makes of their work may be less favorable if they do. Others, who have tenure, think it unwise to complain because they are afraid of being transferred to one of the other, less desirable, schools in the community. Still other teachers dislike disagreeing with anyone and would tolerate a great deal without complaining. A few are so impressed with the status leader's good intentions and sincerity that they are reluctant to voice any objections. One teacher, who is definitely hoping for an appointment as assistant to the status leader, feels it would not be wise to express his opposition.

Although force, as it is described here, is generally frowned upon in educational circles, it is often used. Whether or not it is being used as a means of influencing the behavior of teachers depends not necessarily on the status leader's intentions but rather on the way his actions are viewed by the teachers. And their awareness that force is being used is not usually freely expressed. They are likely, however, to feel that they are being coerced when decisions are rushed, or when a status leader is required to take certain actions without consulting his staff, or when he assumes he already knows the best method of working or the best action to take.

In the illustration just given there may have been disagreement between the status leader and the teachers about both goals and means. The teachers may have believed that their instruction was satisfactory, or they may not have realized that the status leader had in mind the goal of improving instruction. They may have recognized his purpose and accepted it but disagreed with the means—reading and reporting on books. In most situations the status leader who presents to his staff a proposal for action rather than a problem needing consideration is likely to be viewed as expecting that his proposal be carried out. The presentation of a proposal for action is interpreted, by many teachers, as an order.

Whenever suggestions from a status leader are not intended as orders but are so interpreted, it is probable that the channels of communication between teachers and status leaders are poor. Often the status leader assumes that everyone will recognize the merit of his proposal and act upon it. He is then surprised to find that some are not wholeheartedly behind his idea but accept it because it is regarded as a command. When he does learn that his behavior is viewed as autocratic by the teachers, he may be hurt. Sometimes he feels that teachers are not cooperative enough and takes retaliatory measures. He may prevent them from doing something they like to do, such as visiting other schools or having time off to attend educational conferences. This, of course, increases rather than alleviates the teachers' suspicions and may set in motion a vicious cycle. Typical consequences are constant criticism of the status leader by teachers and their refusal to put forth substantial effort. If the sense of injustice is keen enough, complete cleavage between administration and teaching staff may result.

The use of force is not possible unless two conditions obtain. First, the status leader must actually have control of many important means needed by teachers to realize their wants—employment, a good working environment, suitable instructional materials, recognition. Second, teachers must control very few, if any, of the means the status leader thinks he needs to achieve his purposes—maintaining himself in a status position, establishing good morale, improving instruction in the school. This seeming imbalance in the control of means is rarely, if ever, in accordance with the facts. In numerous instances a status leader using the method of force in his relations with teachers has literally been forced out of his position because the staff controlled means the status leader believed to be securely within his control. A very few teachers, well entrenched in a community, sometimes have sufficient power to cause a status leader to lose his job.

Bargaining

Administrators and coordinators may influence the behavior of teachers through a kind of bargaining activity in which each trades what he controls for something he needs and the other fellow has. An industrial arts supervisor may bargain with a teacher by informing him that if he will clean up one end of the shop and rack his lumber and supplies in a more orderly fashion, he will get him an added piece of equipment to place in the cleared space. Another industrial arts supervisor may tell a teacher that if he will use plastics and other new materials, he will get him a new lathe and other equipment needed for working with these materials. An English teacher may offer to take two "slow" groups if he is also given an elective class in dramatics. Bargaining implies, "If you'll do this for me, I'll do that for you."

Bargaining need not always be as overt or obvious as it seems to be in these illustrations. Often it is subtle and not recognized for what it is. This way of exercising leadership, if mutual confidence exists, is often better than the method of force. The leader's power is reduced, and the teacher's freedom of choice is increased. Bargaining, however, places serious restrictions on the effectiveness of both teachers and status leaders. Mutual confidence is usually lacking, and a great deal of energy and time is expended by each side in enforcing the bargaining arrangements. Accusations of bad faith are common; and the implication seems to be that the

27

welfare of teachers or status leaders, not that of children, is paramount.

Paternalism

Paternalism is a special case of bargaining in which the bargaining is rarely made explicit. For example, status leaders may want it known that they are doing everything possible to satisfy the needs of teachers, in the hope that teachers will accept their "leadership" out of gratitude and loyalty. This kind of bargaining is widely used, but status leaders are not always fully aware of their "gratitude and loyalty" demands. They may make every effort to improve salary schedules, to obtain sick-leave provisions, to provide rest and recreation rooms, to get the materials teachers want, and otherwise to anticipate teachers' needs. They may perform many small and personal favors for members of their staff. Although no visible strings are attached to such favors, and although there has been no overt bargaining, the official leader is often visibly disappointed by the ingratitude of teachers who subsequently question his policies.

Paternalism has an advantage over the use of force in that it stresses reward rather than punishment. But it also has certain disadvantages. One is the feeling of dependence and inferiority engendered in a teacher who is expected to view the status leader as a beneficent father-figure to whom gratitude and obedience are due. Even the feeling that he should try to carry out the status leader's wishes "because he does so many things for us" or "because he is so good to us" inhibits the teacher and keeps him from making his maximum contribution as an independent and creative individual. He finds it difficult to become a self-respecting professional worker, operating on the basis of intelligence and his own best analysis of a situation. He frequently resents the implication that he is in debt to the status leader. At the same time, he does not want to appear ungrateful for

28

gifts and favors, even though these have not been requested.

The paternalistic method of influencing the behavior of teachers implies, as does the use of force, that teachers and status leaders have different objectives. The official leader helps teachers get what they want so that they, in turn, will help him get what he wants. Paternalism also violates an important psychological principle, which has to do with the sequence of activity and reward. Instead of feeling rewarded for their professional activity, teachers get certain rewards first and then are expected to do what the status leader wants in order to earn the rewards they have already received. This may result in a continuously increasing expectation on the part of teachers. They may want ever-higher salaries or more and better instructional materials without feeling that effort on their part is a prerequisite of such benefits.

Determination of Mutually Acceptable Goals and Means

Status leaders and teachers may work, through free discussion, consultation, and cooperation, to determine common goals and mutually satisfactory ways of achieving these goals. If agreement can be reached on goals, the possibility of discovering mutually satisfactory means is increased. If teachers and their official leader agree, for example, that the teaching of reading needs improvement, securing agreement on possible means of achieving this goal—for example, forming a study group, employing a consultant, or purchasing reading workbooks—becomes easier. The more specifically a problem can be analyzed or a goal identified, the narrower the range of means appearing appropriate to all concerned will be. The understanding individuals have of the various means available and the potential contribution of each naturally influences their selection.

Even if there is no exact agreement on the relative importance of several goals, it may be possible to secure agreement on means. A group of teachers may agree, for example,

29

that reading instruction needs improvement. Although the status leader may not believe that this is the part of the instructional program most deserving of immediate attention, he may be satisfied to have teachers work on improving one important part of the program and cooperate with them in the identification of means acceptable both to him and to them.

The determination of goals and means has been viewed here as an integrated process. Sometimes, however, there is a disposition on the part of official leaders to set the goals and leave the problem of determining means to a staff group. This approach is not likely to meet with success unless there is genuine acceptance of the goals by those who are to determine means. Many examples could be cited of means carelessly selected because of a lack of concern about an imposed goal.

For teachers and status leaders to select mutually acceptable goals and the means of achieving these goals is admittedly difficult. The process appears to necessitate a climate in which status leaders and teachers can work together with mutual trust, in a spirit of free inquiry. When this climate exists, the kind of status leader-teacher relationship that results is often called democratic or cooperative.

As has just been implied, the expression *determination of mutually acceptable goals and means* refers to a relationship between a status leader and one or more of the teachers who work with him. When it is thought of as applying only to a relationship between a status leader and a group, there is danger of misinterpretation. Unless there is genuine unanimity within the group, it is probable that a number of its members will not find the goals and means selected satisfactory. When a status leader and a majority of the group select goals and means satisfactory to them and impose their decision on the minority, the values of mutual goals-means leadership do not exist for the minority.

30

Factors Influencing Status Leader's Selection of Leadership Method

Our discussion of force, bargaining, paternalism, and the determination of mutually acceptable goals and means may have implied that each is used in a planned and studied manner by a particular kind of status leader. This is not likely to be the case. Many status leaders develop their individual pattern of working without much attempt at rationalizing it. Each status leader's pattern may include a combination of two or more ways of exercising leadership, with a characteristic emphasis upon one or more of the four.

In Chapter 1 the influence of psychological climate on the selection of method by a staff group seeking to maintain a core program in spite of parental opposition was considered. Climate also influences status leaders in their selection of goals and means. We found it helpful to differentiate between two aspects of climate, which are not, of course, independent. One is the psychological atmosphere established by the group itself. Parental pressure on a faculty is an illustration of the other—climate established outside the group but affecting group work. It is the effect of this aspect of climate on status leaders that is of interest here.

Whether status leaders use force, bargaining, paternalism, or cooperative determination of goals and means as a method of exercising leadership is not entirely a matter of free choice on their part. As appointed leaders, they are limited by the policy or accepted practice of the total school organization in which they work. The expectations of superiors tend to determine the method status leaders in individual schools will or possibly can use. A superintendent who demands the speedy adaptation of instructional practices to a set policy usually forces the person responsible for these practices in an individual school to use orders and demands in accomplishing the superintendent's goal.

School system policies, if they are enunciated, usually favor "democratic" leadership, or something approaching the determination of mutually acceptable goals and means. Explicitly formulated statements of leadership policy rarely, if ever, recognize force, paternalism, or bargaining, except in situations where unionization of teachers has forced an acceptance of the last. Practice, however, often differs from stated policy and is usually a combination of force, paternalism, bargaining, and the determination of mutually acceptable goals and means. Although principals and coordinators are often told to be "democratic," they also may be expected, on numerous occasions, to overrule staff decisions or obtain staff acceptance of a centrally formulated policy.

A frequent result of intensive lay criticism of the schools is a series of system-wide administrative orders. These orders may require discontinuing the use of a book, dropping a particular kind of card for reporting pupil progress to parents, or giving greater emphasis to the three R's. The orders may be issued even if the practices to be discontinued were developed as the result of a great deal of cooperation among teachers or among teachers and parents. Under such conditions the methods actually used by official leaders in individual schools are determined in large part by the total situation in which they work.

Many other factors in this total situation influence the manner in which status leaders exercise leadership. The expectations of boards of education, parents, and teachers; past practices within the status leader's own school; and practices in other schools within the system are a few of the more important of these. The personal preferences and skills of the status leader at the building level are, of course, also factors in the total working situation. If he wishes to do so, he can usually influence to some extent the forces that tend to limit his choice of leadership methods; and he may ask his superiors or work with his staff to define carefully those areas in which the latter group may reasonably expect to have relative freedom of action.

Superiority of Mutual Goals-Means Leadership

The leadership method involving cooperative identification of mutually acceptable goals and means appeared to us to be superior to other methods on the basis of each of the criteria we developed. First, it increases the possibility of satisfying diverse individual needs simultaneously. One person may seek added knowledge; another, general development as a person; a third, recognition; and a fourth, achievement. Individuals with different needs may, through discussion and planning, agree upon goals and means that will enable each to find satisfaction while working cooperatively with others toward common ends.

Second, leadership stressing the cooperative identification of goals and means is in accordance with what is known about human motivation. This method of exercising leadership is most likely to result in a genuine desire on the part of a staff to work toward improvement of the school program. Cooperative selection of a goal and promising means of achieving that goal increases the sense of personal involvement and responsibility of staff members. An in-service education program focused on problems identified by teachers and conducted in ways they consider helpful generally results in a curriculum superior to that developed when other leadership methods, which ignore or minimize the importance of the positive motivation associated with self-direction, are used. Cooperative identification of mutual goals and mutually acceptable means seems to stimulate learning, growth, and effort on the part of the participants. When status leaders foster this kind of cooperation, much of the lack of effort, resistance to change, and hostility found in many schools tends to disappear.

33

There is increasing recognition that leadership methods that "punish and deny" seldom induce the desired behavior. Instead, they tend to threaten teachers, and this threat usually leads to aggression or withdrawal rather than persistence toward the desired goal. A growing body of evidence suggests that success in changing behavior demands strong emphasis on the kind of leadership that "supports and helps."

The provision of support and help by status leaders means more than the provision of high salaries and other material benefits. It requires the provision of means by which teachers, through their own efforts, are able to achieve increased need-satisfaction. For a status leader to provide means of this kind is not easy. He must be an educator—not a dictator, shrewd bargainer, or benevolent father-figure.

Third, under leadership stressing cooperative selection of goals and means, the potential contributions of the entire staff are most likely to be discovered and used. Because of their training, ability, and experience, teachers are well qualified to work on instructional problems. Establishing goals of value to teachers and status leaders and determining means acceptable to both is the only one of the four kinds of status leader-teacher relationships that permits full utilization of the potential contribution of every member of the group.

A frequent objection to the mutual goals-means approach to the solution of instructional problems is that it reduces the control of the official leader, and hence his power or authority. Actually, his power is not reduced. The official leader's power is dependent on the extent to which he controls means others desire to use, and the means he controls are not modified. However, he is limited in the use of his power, or in the use of the means he controls. For example, his official position may have invested him with the power to dismiss a teacher, or to recommend a teacher's transfer, or to block a salary increase. If he is genuinely interested in

34

fostering the development of mutual goals and mutually acceptable means, he will not use these powers. He will support and help teachers, not punish them or deny them the goals they want to achieve or the means they want to use.

If the official leader is to use the mutual goals-means approach to curriculum improvement, he must choose between a policy of support, suggestion, and approval and a policy of order, threat, demand, and punishment. If (1) teachers are dependent on the status leader for important means and (2) their objectives and methods do not correspond with those he values, they are likely to feel threatened and inhibited to some extent even if the status leader does not use the powers he possesses. Often, before a staff is willing to risk the status leader's displeasure by discussing problems and solutions freely, he must demonstrate by his behavior, and for some time, that he will not order, demand, threaten, or punish.

Status Leader's Role in
Mutual Goals-Means Leadership

There is little doubt that status leaders can increase the frequency with which goals and means are cooperatively identified. They must, however, exert conscious effort to encourage the participation of staff members, and they must give teachers the help they need to carry out their plans.

Teachers and status leaders must derive personal satisfactions from activities that further the purposes of the schools. Naturally, their needs are varied; they may include the need for participation, for recognition, for achievement, and for status. When teachers are genuinely involved in planning the school program and in planning means of overcoming the inadequacies they perceive, they usually report satisfaction of many of these needs. Representative committees, total staff meetings, study groups, workshops—all

35

provide opportunities for involvement in planning through cooperative determination of goals and means. They tend to foster staff initiative, creativeness, adaptability, flexibility, and willingness to experiment—qualities necessary for the development of instructional programs of high quality.

It may be helpful to describe here, in general terms, some of the activities the status leader who desires to stimulate the cooperative determination of goals and means will probably engage in. In the course of his work on instructional problems with one or more staff members, he will probably provide help in identifying goals, exploring and identifying means, and using and testing means; and he will do all he can to further the development of staff initiative and self-reliance. In an actual working situation the steps would not, of course, be as orderly or discrete as they may appear to be in the following presentation.

Identifying Goals

Before mutually acceptable means can be determined, goals that both the status leader and the staff member or members value must be identified. The goals may relate to many areas; they may include such matters as the study of drop-outs, the development of a homeroom plan, or the initiation of a core program.

There are at least two prerequisites of goal identification that is genuinely cooperative. First, the status leader must make clear to staff members that he is not a threat to them, that he will not overrule them, and that he will not penalize them for statements made or ideas expressed. Only then does it become possible for the staff to recognize him as a possible source of help in solving instructional problems. The initiative in creating this kind of relationship must usually be taken by the status leader. Whether or not he succeeds will depend, in part, upon his actual position in the school organization and on the staff's perception of his role. He will have to make clear, by word and deed, his desire to work toward the goals that are of genuine concern to individuals and to the group as a whole. He might well express with great circumspection his own ideas concerning the appropriateness of a specific goal until it is apparent that his statements will not deter members from expressing their views.

Second, those identifying the goals must be clearly aware of what a particular goal really means to them. The status leader can help them achieve this awareness. For example, a group decision to study the problem of drop-outs—to try to discover why boys and girls leave school—may have many different meanings for individual members. In one staff group that had made such a decision some of the teachers were anxious to find ways of reducing student mortality; others believed that the study would result in justification of the present program and would make proposed curriculum changes unnecessary; still others believed that many young people who were being retained in school should be dropped. If this variation in point of view had been recognized from the beginning, it would have markedly influenced the nature of the study that was undertaken.

Information about the particular situations or conditions—as these are perceived by staff members—leading to the identification of a certain goal is exceedingly useful. Also helpful is information concerning the results individuals expect from their work toward the goal. When, as in the illustration just cited, there are obvious differences in expectation, these must be given careful attention during the study if expectations are to be fulfilled and consensus or even mutual understanding reached. Often individuals are pessimistic about the possibility of solving certain problems. Previous failures are reported, or doubts concerning the possibility of obtaining needed administrative support are expressed. If such barriers to enthusiastic effort can be removed, progress toward the goal is facilitated.

During the exploratory process it is helpful for the status leader to clarify and try to communicate his own perception of the goal, his related needs and objectives, his responsibilities, and the kind of help he believes he can give the group. The danger, however, is that he will present not only his analysis of the problem but also his solution. If the status leader of the group trying to discover why boys and girls leave school had strongly implied that the only sensible thing to do was to keep in school all children who were physically able, those holding a different view might have been deterred from making their position known. The status leader who refrains from stating his solution to a problem but attempts to maneuver the staff so that his solution will ultimately be accepted also defeats the purpose of a cooperative examination of possible goals and means. Although he may advisably present his experience and views in the process of exploring a situation or goal, he must make every effort to avoid having his contribution accepted because of his status. There must be free and sincere inquiry if the purpose of the exploration—selection and clarification of goals—is to be achieved.

Exploring and Identifying Means

The identification of means that are acceptable to both staff and status leader is often a difficult process. It is especially likely to prove difficult if, as in the example involving the study of drop-outs, the meaning of the goal for individual staff members has not been clarified. However, if several possible approaches to the attainment of agreed-upon goals are carefully and cooperatively examined, not only appropriate means—those likely to result in achievement of the goal—but also means that are mutually satisfactory—means likely to meet the needs of the staff as well as those of the status leader—can usually be identified.

The status leader can assist in the exploration and identifi-

38

cation of means by helping to develop a climate that encourages individual and cooperative thought, decision, and action. He may introduce factual data, suggest procedures for attacking a problem, or otherwise communicate his own ideas. He must, however, introduce ideas in such a way that the staff will regard the proposals as tentative, not definitive or coercive. This approach may imply to some that the status leader should compromise with what he regards best. Although it is true that he will constantly find it necessary to weigh values, there is no implication that he should sacrifice his integrity. He must try to conduct himself in such a way as to further most effectively the aims of the school. He may have to give up, at least temporarily, the means he regards best; but there is a strong probability that through a cooperative approach in which the resources of the group are utilized, even better means will be identified. Whatever ways of achieving the goal are suggested, they are of little value unless they are considered pertinent and helpful by the staff members who will be doing the actual work.

Identifying mutually acceptable means is often more difficult than identifying mutually acceptable goals. Individuals frequently have a preference for specific means—methods, resources, or ways of working—as a result of previous experience or previously developed skills. The fact that evidence concerning the relative merit of several different means is often lacking of course makes the problem of choosing among them more difficult.

Using and Testing Means

It is often difficult to put into practice the method of achieving a goal that has been selected. New procedures to be used in conducting meetings or new methods of working with students may have to be learned. Teachers may feel insecure unless opportunities are provided to develop these new methods or to perfect those only partially developed.

39

The status leader can help to reduce or prevent this kind of insecurity. He may be able to help staff members anticipate difficulties and plan for them adequately. He may be able to help them analyze problems or practice needed skills. He may be able to aid them in making a sound evaluation of the consequences of their actions. By helping individuals and staff groups to maintain perspective regarding immediate and long-term activities, and by helping to coordinate the efforts of various individuals, he can foster stable and balanced progress toward mutual goals. By providing support before, during, and after the testing of agreed-upon means, the status leader can stimulate increased self-direction and competence on the part of the staff. Modification of means may, of course, be needed after trial and experience, and this modification again becomes the joint responsibility of the official leader and the staff group.

Developing Staff Initiative and Self-Reliance

The task of mobilizing staff efforts and abilities for effective instruction in a sense defines an intermediate goal for the status leader. This goal is to help teachers assume responsibility for employing the agreed-upon means and for achieving the agreed-upon goals. Although the status leader is also involved in working toward these goals, his ultimate purpose is to improve the total school program. The idea that instruction can be improved only as teachers themselves learn how to improve their methods and techniques means, in effect, that teachers must accept responsibility for the improvement of instruction. There may be considerable difficulty in securing acceptance of this responsibility by a staff group.

The importance of a permissive atmosphere, which encourages staff initiative in identifying goals, exploring and identifying means, and using and testing means, becomes clear once the importance of self-reliance on the part of the

40

staff is recognized. If the staff is too dependent on the status leader, unrealistic demands are likely to be made upon him, and he may be blamed for failures. Of course, if he provides significant assistance, some measure of dependence is almost inevitable. There is a delicate balance between appropriate and inappropriate dependence. This balance is most likely to be achieved if the status leader keeps clearly in mind his goal of helping staff members to modify their values, understandings, and skills in order to work cooperatively for the achievement of cooperatively identified goals.

Summary

This chapter has elaborated the conception of leadership presented in Chapter 1 and has described four methods of exercising leadership: force, bargaining, paternalism, and the determination of mutually acceptable goals and means. The last method was favored for several reasons. First, it offers the greatest opportunity for satisfying diverse individual needs. Second, it appears to be sound psychologically. It provides for maximum motivation and self-direction on the part of staff members, and self-direction is essential to the learning and growth of professional workers. Cooperative determination of goals and means appears, too, to minimize the resistance to change prevalent when other leadership methods are used. Third, the development of mutually desirable goals and means is democratic in that this method of exercising leadership not only takes into account the needs of the greatest number of individuals but gives promise of their maximum contribution. Full development of and respect for every person is more likely to result.

There is a fourth consideration, already implied, which further supports instructional leadership involving cooperative determination of goals and means. When the curriculum is thought of as the experiences learners have under the direction of the school, improvement in the curriculum requires that these experiences become better ones. There is rather widespread acceptance of the idea that this can happen only as the people responsible for the experiences improve their values, understandings and skills, and relations with one another. Leadership that stresses the cooperative development of goals and means appears to be most conducive to the growth and development of individuals, to the establishment of democratic relationships, and to the free and constructive exchange of ideas.

3

PEOPLE AS SITUATIONAL FACTORS AFFECTING LEADERSHIP

As we have stated a number of times, instructional leadership is conditioned by a large number of situational factors.[1] That is, the nature of the specific situation largely determines what the leader can and should do. Some of these situational factors were considered in Chapters 1 and 2. In this chapter we are concerned primarily with people and the relations among them as factors in any situation in which leadership is exercised. We discuss the implications of (1) differences among individuals involved in a working situation; (2) relations among these individuals; and (3) school organization, both formal and informal. We also suggest a number of things status leaders can do to facilitate a mutual goals-means approach to curriculum improvement.

Individual Differences

In all the schools in which we were working we found that individual differences among staff members were great.

[1] In our analysis of situational factors we received considerable help from a book by John M. Pfiffner entitled *The Supervision of Personnel* (New York, Prentice-Hall, Inc., 1951).

We found, too, that unless people with status leadership responsibilities constantly studied, as individuals, the teachers with whom they worked, the kind of leadership we considered desirable was not likely to be developed.

Although it is true that the people we worked with were alike in many ways, our tendency was to exaggerate the common elements and pay less than sufficient attention to the differences. These differences involved motivation for work, abilities, skills, understandings, needs, attitudes, temperament, work pace, emotional stability, gregariousness, and disposition to accept and benefit from criticism. We realized that the basis for these differences might be hereditary as well as environmental; but, regardless of their origin, recognizing their existence helped us to understand why particular individuals often functioned better in one job than in another. We learned that leadership was more effective when these differences were taken into consideration in job placement or work adjustment.

Differences among teachers as well as status leaders can be dealt with intelligently only when they are recognized, analyzed, and understood. Recognizing and understanding differences, however, is extremely difficult. We found, for example, that it took us a long time to reach even a partial understanding of the different attitudes held by members of our staffs toward their work and toward us.

Motivation for Work

Prior to the leadership project some of us tended to view the professional motivation of the teachers we were associated with as resulting almost entirely from external influences in the form of rewards and punishments. We were likely, that is, to explain motivation primarily in terms of financial payments and threats to security. Our study, however, led us to believe that such an explanation was a gross oversimplification. The extent to which salaries serve

44

to motivate work depends, among other things, on the cultural background of the individuals concerned and on their expectations regarding income. Similarly, although fear certainly is a motivating influence, we came to believe that fear of what is believed to be arbitrary action by others is destructive and leads to results neither desired nor expected. This kind of fear, of course, is different from what may be regarded as normal apprehension resulting from the recognition of having made a mistake. Fear in this latter sense is common and may frequently act as a deterrent to further mistakes. However, it appeared to us that security, or freedom from threat, is much more conducive to creative and cooperative problem solving than fear. Freedom from threat encourages the constructive and responsible contribution of staff members. Security makes curricular experimentation possible.

Most surveys of the attitude people have toward their work indicate that opportunities to participate in problem solving, a feeling that their opinions are considered, comfortable working conditions, a good boss or supervisor, and an opportunity for advancement are all more important than salary—assuming a reasonable minimum—in motivating work. Many of the factors individuals regard as important in developing a favorable attitude toward their work relate to their feelings of personal worth and self-esteem. Our studies and thought and discussion tended to corroborate these findings. The job satisfaction of teachers and status leaders is affected more by the social and individual satisfactions they derive from their work than by administrative policies and regulations. And the principal or other building status leader is in a favorable position to increase the social satisfactions teachers get from their work and from their associations with their peers.

Motivation for work is influenced by many factors, and individuals differ widely in respect to what motivates them.

Although learning about the specific conditions that motivate a particular individual is always difficult, even incomplete information can be of help to the status leader who is trying to encourage the determination of mutually desirable goals and means.

In trying to gain some understanding of our own motivation and that of our associates, we frequently overlooked the fact that human beings act on the basis of emotion as well as reason. Rationality is only one aspect of man's behavior. Much of what we and our associates did could not be explained on the basis of a careful weighing of facts and a reasonable choice between alternatives. What seems reasonable to one individual may seem very unreasonable to another. For example, it might be assumed that merit rating, with higher salaries paid to those with greater abilities, should appeal to everyone. Yet it is well known that, in general, teachers want uniform pay for equal experience and training. To cite another example: It is undoubtedly difficult for an exuberant young teacher who wants to put pupils on their own to understand an older teacher who believes that pupils have become increasingly irresponsible. Similarly, some of the older teachers probably have difficulty in understanding the position of the younger ones. Each group may seem to the other to be behaving in an irrational way.

In the course of the leadership project we discussed many kinds of individual differences, all affecting relations between a group and its leaders. The important conclusion reached was that until official leaders recognize the great differences among individuals and seek to understand them, the foundation for cooperative work will be insecure. We recognized that the major significance of differences among individuals is their effect on the way people react to situations. And we found that as we observed how an individual responded to situations whose elements we could identify, we began to gain an understanding of that individual.

Conception of Roles

We realized that a group of status leaders would illustrate all the individual differences already mentioned in connection with teachers. Early in the Denver project we gave considerable attention to our differing conceptions of our own leadership roles, and we found this helpful in clarifying our ideas about leadership.

In one of the early group sessions we identified the following functions of a leader: (1) cooperating with others in the identification of mutually acceptable goals; (2) stimulating individual and cooperative decision, action, and evaluation; (3) developing a favorable climate for individual and group effort; (4) guiding individuals and groups toward greater self-direction and competence; (5) helping individuals and groups to maintain perspective regarding immediate and long-range activities; (6) providing individuals and groups with needed guidance and resources at appropriate times; (7) coordinating the efforts of others; (8) carrying out effectively any responsibilities for action that have been accepted. We learned subsequently that these words meant various things to us and that the practices implied by these functions were hard to learn. Later in our work, as we elaborated our ideas about leadership, we saw that the official leader's conception of his role had much to do with determining whether or not he actually was or could become a leader who fostered the cooperative development of goals and means.

In the course of the project we gave extensive attention to leadership practices. These were not always carefully scrutinized, however, for consistency with our conception of good leadership. As a result, we did not fully grasp the implications of certain practices while we were engaged in them. We did recognize, however, that the situations in which specific techniques were used, as well as our skill

47

in using them, were important in determining whether or not we achieved true mutual goals-means leadership.

Until we were well into the project we often recognized only vaguely the need for specific leadership techniques and skills. Had our work continued longer, many of these would have received more attention. For example, our discussion of the importance of differences in perception impressed many individuals with the necessity of developing skill in ascertaining the perceptions of others. Although many of us, as status leaders, had long sought to develop a constructive, healthy, working situation, we came to realize that the way individual staff members perceived this situation was of primary importance. As we worked, it became evident that skill in self-analysis and ability to analyze the motivation of others were also required. We recognized the importance of assessing the impact of situational factors we were sure were operating and realized we lacked the skills necessary for this task. We came, too, to recognize the need for skill in analyzing the influence of our own practices on our colleagues.

Perception and Behavior

In considering what status leaders might do to deal more effectively with situational factors pertaining to the individuals involved in a working situation, we gave primary attention to the significance of perceptions. Throughout the Denver project we tried to increase our sensitivity to the way our co-workers regarded themselves and us and their work. Sensitivity to the perceptions of others seemed to us to be essential to leadership. We realized that we frequently failed to perceive and understand our own motives, goals, stereotypes, and attitudes. We found it even more difficult to recognize and understand those of others.

Our exploration of the relation between perception and behavior led eventually to the formulation of a statement concerning the implications of differences in perception for educational leadership. The statement, which is summarized below, listed and illustrated six major points.[2]

1. Particularly as it involves relations with others, most behavior can be explained as an attempt to achieve or preserve integrity and maintain or enhance self-esteem. Almost everything a person does has some direct bearing on his feelings of personal worth. This concept helped us, as educational leaders, to understand both our own behavior and that of the teachers with whom we worked. In our opinion, one of the reasons for much of the misunderstanding between teachers and status leaders is that neither group knows very much about what enhances the self-esteem of the other. Everyone willingly engages in activities that maintain or increase his self-esteem and resists or avoids those that have the opposite effect. To work successfully in cooperation with others, a person must know at least something about the kinds of situations and activities that contribute to the feelings of worth of his associates.

2. Behavior is determined by the individual's perceptions of the total situation and its requirements. These perceptions are highly personal, differing from individual to individual. An instructional leader, or anyone else for that matter, must develop sensitivity to the perceptions of others if communication and interpersonal relations are to be improved. The same words frequently have very different meanings for different persons. For example, a curriculum coordinator might meet two teachers in the corridor and say to both simultaneously, "I would like to be of help, if I can, in connection with those arithmetic units you are working on."

[2] See Stephen M. Corey, Arthur W. Foshay, and Gordon N. Mackenzie, "Instructional Leadership and the Perceptions of the Individuals Involved," *The Bulletin of the National Association of Secondary-School Principals*, 35:83–91, November 1951.

One of the teachers might think, "He's being thoughtful and wants me to know that he's interested in my work and would like to help." The coordinator's comments might mean something quite different to the other teacher, whose unspoken reaction might be, "What has he heard about my arithmetic units? I think they're good. He should wait until his help is requested."

3. *At the time of action a person does what seems justified by his view of the situation.* It is difficult to accept and act in accordance with this idea. An examination of past behavior always reveals instances of foolish behavior, and it is embarrassing to admit that at the time they occurred, subsequently acknowledged mistakes were considered correct and proper actions. However, once it is realized that any action, at the time of its occurrence, is regarded as justifiable by the person acting, there is less likelihood that anyone will be suspected of deliberately doing something he himself realizes at the time he should not do. Suspicion of this kind leads to blame, threat, and punishment, and these make impossible the kind of relationship between status leaders and their associates that is conducive to productive work.

4. *People react differently to the same situation because each person's perception of the situation differs from that of the others.* The reaction of the teacher who sees the status leader primarily as a person who evaluates him and notes his strengths and weaknesses will be different from that of the teacher who sees the status leader as a person who is anxious to help him and give him support. Each of these two teachers, although reacting to what may objectively be the "same" status leader, perceives him differently. In making this statement, we realize that the way an individual perceives—that is, sizes up and interprets—a situation in which he is involved depends, among other things, on his background and experience, on the presence or absence of emotional blocks,

and on the time he has to organize and differentiate among his perceptions before action is necessary.

5. *Most people feel satisfaction when they realize that their perceptions and consequent behavior are considered correct by other members of the group or groups to which they want to belong.* Most teachers who are proud of their profession feel satisfaction when they know that their perceptions are similar to those of their professional associates. Everyone derives satisfaction from being accepted by a group, and most people believe that their view of a situation is realistic and correct if it is consistent with the way those of their associates whom they admire interpret the same situation.

6. *Changed perceptions lead to changed behavior.* We thought this concept had many implications for improving relations between instructional leaders and teachers. If the status leader believes that teachers should react differently to a certain kind of teaching situation, he should do whatever he can to enable them to extend, clarify, and differentiate among their perceptions of that situation. Sometimes a teacher can, through discussion, become aware of certain important elements of a situation—elements whose significance he has previously ignored or minimized for one reason or another. Whether or not the discussion is effective in creating this awareness depends largely on the extent to which it is interpreted by the teacher as threatening. Other methods of extending perceptions of a particular teaching situation include reading, experimentation, and additional firsthand experience with similar situations.

As we discussed the foregoing statement about perception, we realized that we did not know very much about how we might improve our ability to see things through another person's eyes. Certainly, if anyone is to feel free to talk

51

directly about the way he sees things, he must have a substantial amount of faith in the good intentions of those to whom he is speaking. However, the expression of the way a situation appears to a person is often indirect. Complaints, praise, and plans are all based on an interpretation of the situation by those who are complaining or praising or planning.

Many perceptions are not, of course, expressed verbally at all but manifest themselves in bodily movements, facial expressions, or significant silences. There are many levels of perception, ranging from the conscious recognition of what is plainly present in a situation to an unconscious reaction to elements unconsciously recognized. Much of the behavior of both educational leaders and teachers is symptomatic of such unconscious recognition. When one feels tense during a professional conference without knowing why, or sees another person become tense, it is likely that the unconscious recognition of threat is at work. Lacking the psychiatrist's skill, we decided that we could only wait sympathetically for the person to solve the problem himself or get it out into the open so that it could be attacked cooperatively. The cooperative approach can often achieve results in time, provided the relationship among the people involved is nonthreatening.

Abilities and Needs

In the course of our consideration of how status leaders might effectively use the different skills, attitudes, and abilities of individuals in specific situations, we developed an increased awareness of the importance of providing a variety of personnel services. Discharging instructional leadership responsibilities through determination of mutually acceptable goals and means seemed to us to necessitate close attention to the needs and abilities of staff members.

It is often assumed that the personnel services of a school

system are better performed by central office workers than by principals and building curriculum coordinators. Although status leaders at the building level may or may not participate in the original selection and placement of teachers, we came to believe that they should have continuing responsibility for teacher guidance, counseling, and evaluation, and for interpersonal relations in general. This responsibility is closely related to the instructional leadership function of principals and curriculum coordinators, because the official leaders' relations with staff groups determine whether or not a mutual goals-means approach to the solution of instructional problems is possible.

Although instructional leaders often overlook the specific needs of individual teachers in their efforts to deal with the more obvious, concrete, practical problems of curriculum improvement, in-service education offers many opportunities for meeting these needs. The group procedures necessary for the cooperative determination of goals and means may provide group therapy, whether or not it is so labeled. A full realization of the group-therapy potential, however, depends largely on the understanding and skill of status leaders. In-service education can help clarify goals, widen areas of understanding, and improve skills. It offers opportunities for group guidance and job adjustment. We recognized that our explorations in this area were tentative, but we felt confident that much good could result from viewing in-service education as an integral part of the personnel services of a school system.

Teacher rating is a responsibility frequently assigned to a building status leader. He often resists this assignment because it almost inevitably precludes the free and permissive relationship necessary for genuinely cooperative work on curriculum problems. Teachers do not like to be rated, and many find it difficult if not impossible to work freely with the person responsible for periodically evaluating them. It seemed to us, however, that some methods of evaluating teachers overcome many of the difficulties inherent in the usual rating procedures. A periodic conference with the official leader, during which the teacher's professional needs are discussed and he is encouraged to suggest his own program of in-service education, is quite different from the usual rating. The teacher may be helped to clarify his ultimate educational objectives and to outline the manner in which he hopes to achieve them.

Some of us experimented successfully with descriptive reports of teaching performance in place of the usual rating procedures. We felt, too, that more extensive use might well be made of a placement, or guidance, approach. This means that the abilities of staff members are analyzed, with their cooperation and help, not in order to rank them on a competitive basis but to guide them and place them in the position for which they are best suited. Because teachers and jobs vary considerably, it is often true that the individual who does not succeed in certain kinds of activity can succeed in others. The process of analysis, guidance, and adjustment may be informal, and it may be carried on quite incidentally in a free working situation if there is good communication and rapport between status leader and teachers. A guidance approach to teacher evaluation appeared to us to be essential to intelligent and truly cooperative work on school problems.

School systems often have provisions for transferring teachers from one school to another if their work is unsatisfactory or if they are not happy with their assignment. Clearly, transfer to another school may be a means of securing better adjustment. However, transfers often tend to become a disciplinary device rather than an adjustment service, and they in no way help the individual to operate more effectively in the new situation. By transferring teachers, status leaders sometimes pass their problems on to someone else. This may shift them geographically, but that is all.

Schools have made great progress in providing guidance services for pupils. They have made much less progress in providing appropriate guidance services for staff members. We learned that if we, as official leaders, expected to render assistance to the people with whom we worked, we had to study them as individuals. Although many problems can be handled through group work, this approach did not seem to us to be adequate for all personnel problems and adjustments. In exploring guidance techniques that might be used by building status leaders, we found that counseling that was quite nondirective often helped people to reach a better understanding of themselves and their work. Some of us, of course, found it difficult to be nondirective. We frequently were expected to supply answers.

There were other reasons that tended to prevent us from using a guidance approach at all, and some of these are not difficult to identify. The provision of personnel services has not been widely accepted as an assigned function of building leaders, primarily because the relation between these services and effective instructional leadership has not been carefully explored. In addition, there are often personal reasons that discourage building leaders from rendering personnel services to members of their staff. Some of us admitted frankly that we were ill at ease when we had to listen to teachers talk about their personal difficulties. There is probably a tendency to avoid implying acceptance of responsibility for the personal problems of staff members, regardless of whether the problems are those of the well-adjusted person or those of someone who appears to be seriously maladjusted. Many of us felt that we lacked the skills necessary for dealing at all adequately with personal problems.

The building leader who tries sincerely to counsel with teachers will, at times, find himself in situations he would prefer to avoid. We realized, however, that the personal problems of teachers influence the kind of leadership possible in a school situation and that serious emotional problems of teachers or status leaders menace the social equilibrium of the entire school. The status leader, therefore, must learn to recognize his own problems and needs and to help teachers recognize and meet theirs.

The guidance approach to personnel problems does not imply that every instructional leader should be trained in psychiatry or social work. It does imply a willingness on his part to face rather than run away from the personal problems of staff members. A number of relatively simple procedures and materials can help the status leader become aware of what these problems are. We found post-meeting reaction questionnaires especially helpful in connection with identifying personal problems in group work situations.

It goes almost without saying that calmness and a considerable degree of emotional maturity are essential to successful counseling of any variety. We were convinced, however, that even though the status leader possessed these qualities, the problems brought to him would, at times, be beyond his ability to handle effectively. He should therefore know how, when, and to whom to send his colleagues for special help.

Interpersonal Relations

In this section various aspects of interpersonal relations are considered as situational factors affecting mutual goals-means leadership. Although the influence they exert may vary, we believe that they all, to a certain extent, enter into every situation in which leadership is being exercised. Many of our observations concerning the effect of interpersonal relations on leadership appeared to us to be in harmony with the findings of social psychologists and the results of studies of interpersonal relations in business and industry. However, there have been few analogous studies involving instructional situations in schools, and we believe that there is great potential value in further investigations of this entire area.

Psychological Climate[3]

As we examined various situational factors affecting mutual goals-means leadership, we were impressed again and again by the importance of the psychological climate in which a staff group operates. We became increasingly aware, for example, of how important a feeling of security is for productive work. Real or imagined threats to the satisfaction of needs often caused what seemed to be irrational behavior, or at least the interruption of harmonious, cooperative effort. As we have already said, we realized that it was the individual staff member's perception of the psychological climate that was important, and that perceptions of a particular situation varied from individual to individual.

We noted that the approval and support of official leaders seemed to be essential to security, good morale, and high standards of work. Absence of approval often led to suspicion, resistance, or antagonism. This does not imply that everything everyone does must meet with expressions of approval. The commendation must be sincere and discriminating. Many of us realized, however, that unless definite attention is given to the importance of expressing approval, good work is likely to be taken for granted, and comments may be made only when work is poor.

We observed that understanding of school policies, philosophy, requirements, duties, and regulations; knowledge of the functions of various staff members; and information about anticipated changes that might affect an individual were all of great significance in developing security. Consistency on the part of official leaders in respect to policies,

[3] Our thinking in this area was influenced by an article by Douglas McGregor entitled "Conditions of Effective Leadership in the Industrial Organizations," *Journal of Consulting Psychology*, 8:55–63, 1944.

point of view, and basis for support of staff members was also important.

Patterns of Participation

As we began to pay more and more attention to the attitudes of our co-workers, we noted that those who felt secure tended to exercise initiative more frequently and to be more independent in their actions—to utilize their abilities and skills in such a way as to derive greater satisfaction from their work. Growth in individual resourcefulness and independence was most clearly observable when staff members had numerous opportunities to participate in planning, to express ideas, and to contribute suggestions about aspects of the instructional program that involved or interested them.

Many of us observed, too, that as staff members participated, through discussion or in other ways, their desire or willingness to accept responsibility seemed to increase—although individual differences were, of course, great. We interpreted this increased disposition to accept responsibility as a further indication of growth in self-reliance; and we concluded that most individuals will in time accept or even seek responsibility if they do not feel threatened and if responsibility is not thrust upon them before they are ready for it.

We recognized that there were distinct differences from school to school in degree and quality of staff participation in the affairs of the school. Some staff groups might be involved in planning their own classroom teaching; others, in planning the over-all program for the entire school. In some schools participation was very informal and relatively unplanned, taking the form of slips placed in a suggestion box. Individuals were encouraged to make suggestions, but little was done to put them into effect unless a proposal happened to impress the official leader. In other schools the suggestion box was supplemented or supplanted by a system of consultation. Status leaders would habitually consult with, or seek advice from, individuals whose judgment they respected or who were members of appointed or elected advisory councils. In some schools there was a very close working relationship between all teachers and official leaders. Areas in which improvement was needed were jointly determined, and the entire staff worked to achieve agreed-upon goals. In other schools, even though status leaders and teachers appeared to have difficulty in communicating with one another, some procedures that helped the latter group to make positive suggestions for improvement were being employed.

We found that meetings—whether of the entire staff, or of subgroups, or of committees—could be effectively used to increase teacher involvement in planning. Meetings may, of course, merely be opportunities for listening even when there is a sincere desire on the part of official leaders to bring about widespread participation. We found that at times many of us engaged in practices that actually discouraged participation. Excessive talking by the official leader, his decision to leave opportunities for participation until the end of the meeting, when everyone is ready to leave, his tendency to be dogmatic—these are only three of the practices that are likely to inhibit the participation of staff members.

Our experience suggested that the pattern of participation to which a group has been accustomed has a great deal of influence on the possibility of developing what we have called mutual goals-means instructional leadership. Before this kind of leadership can be effective, working groups must develop both the desire to participate and the skills necessary for participation. The instructional leader who recognizes that this is true can do much to provide a variety of opportunities both for participation and the learning of participation skills.

Attitudes and Beliefs

Another aspect of interpersonal relations that impressed us as influencing leadership was the tendency toward fixed attitudes and beliefs relating to the behavior of other people. Frequently these beliefs and attitudes persist even when they are contradicted by events.

In some school systems persistent and destructive attitudes toward one another have been developed by status leaders in buildings and status leaders in the central office. For example, some building leaders feel that central office instructional workers are too theoretical and impractical and do not understand the problems of the individual schools. Such an attitude, which tends to preclude real cooperation, is likely to be developed when central office workers impose instructional programs on individual schools. This practice means that the judgment of the building status leader is frequently overruled, and he may feel that his authority is less than he had been led to believe it was. He may accuse the central office workers of being ignorant of the conditions he has to cope with when they insist that he implement a program he believes to be quite unworkable in his school. If this kind of conflict develops, the principal may try to make the central office personnel believe he is doing what is expected of him, when actually he is only going through the motions.

The belief almost directly opposite to that just described is also quite prevalent. Some principals and building curriculum coordinators feel that central office workers are too preoccupied with petty details and routines—not interested enough in educational theory and "big" ideas for curriculum improvement.

Another belief instructional leaders at the individual school level can easily acquire is that they are the authorities in their own school and any questioning of this authority by teachers is an instance of insubordination. The questioner is labeled an obstructionist. Some men and women who rise to official leadership positions in school systems have strong paternalistic tendencies. They are self-assured, and they believe that the successful leader is one who can make up his mind quickly and get other people to carry out his decisions with a minimum of friction. Such instructional leaders are disturbed when their judgment is questioned or criticized; and they are likely to be suspicious of any approach to work that is based on consultation, development of mutually acceptable goals and means, and free two-way communication between teachers and status leaders.

Some central office workers have a stereotyped conception of building status leaders. The supervisor may read carefully the literature dealing with curriculum improvement and development at the individual school level and identify himself with the more recent speculations and theories. In part, perhaps, because he is not responsible for actually implementing the new ideas, he is likely to become impatient with building status leaders and to regard them as reactionary, or stubborn, or uncooperative, or slow to learn.

One attitude many teachers have toward official leaders received a great deal of discussion. This attitude is one of deep-seated fear and distrust. It probably accounts for some of the widespread opposition to rating schemes and salary schedules based on merit ratings. It also explains why some teachers develop a great desire to "tell off" administrators. Because they are afraid or suspicious, they find it necessary to demonstrate forcefully their courage and independence.

In a number of schools some teachers have adopted the attitude that it is a sign of immaturity to express enthusiasm for "extra" work or to do it unless one is forced to. This attitude precludes any real sharing of responsibilities. The new teacher who is believed to be too interested in curriculum improvement activities may be subjected to social pressures to make him conform to the group attitude toward meetings and curriculum study in general.

A negative attitude toward improvement of teaching procedures often results when all proposals for curriculum study come from the administration and are felt by teachers to threaten their security. Frequently the introduction of new courses or the reorganization of the curriculum is strongly resisted. Some teachers interpret the new program as growing out of the administrator's covert and unfavorable evaluation of their work, and therefore as an implied criticism.

The official leader at the individual school level who desires to deal effectively with such pervasive attitudes or beliefs as those just described might well start by trying to understand his own beliefs and attitudes. We found that status leaders who seemed to have few fixed attitudes toward or beliefs about other people were more successful in their work with teachers and other official leaders than those who seemed to have a great many. However, there tends to be some conflict of stereotyped beliefs in all areas of school activity. Even within a single school some teachers are inclined to blame administrators for lack of progress and some administrators are inclined to blame teachers for the same fault, even though the facts may support neither attitude. Recognition of the existence of certain attitudes and an understanding of their psychological significance will help to bring about better interpersonal relations and make possible more effective leadership.

Conflict, Rivalry, and Tension

Conflict, tension, and rivalry characterize all groups to a certain extent, at certain times, and groups of school people are no exception. Conflict usually grows out of various threats—real or imagined—to security. Sometimes the conflict appears quite irrational to outsiders. Often it springs up between people whose interests are closely allied. For ex-

62

ample, the opinions of general education teachers concerning desirable teacher-student relations may conflict with those of vocational education teachers. Conflict may develop between the public and a teaching staff over the use of certain instructional materials or over methods of teaching. In many schools there is more or less constant conflict between some teachers and their pupils.

Considerable tension may develop among individuals and groups as a result of differences in point of view. In the field of education these differences may relate to goals, but they are more likely to relate to means of achieving agreed-upon goals. For example, a controversy may develop over whether a particular project should emphasize cooperative planning or group work techniques.

Hostilities may result from improper placement of personnel within the school system. In some instances there may be a struggle for power between two individuals, and those caught in the middle may be hurt. The desire to be appointed to the chairmanship of a department, or to an assistant-principalship or principalship, often leads to rivalry and conflict. In some school systems the unionization of teachers has resulted in a great many conflicts. Many of these have developed because of the difficulty of determining the prerogatives of teachers' unions and school administrations.

Although a certain amount of conflict is probably inevitable because a core of real disagreement may remain after confusions and ambiguities in communication have been reduced to a minimum, we observed that much of the conflict that interferes with cooperative work results from insecurity or lack of sufficient information or understanding. It appeared to us that there are several prerequisites of a substantial reduction in conflict and that these are similar to the prerequisites of a truly cooperative determination of goals and means. Among them are (1) adequate two-way communication between teachers and status leaders; (2) teacher participation in policy development; (3) genuine concern on the part of the administration for the welfare of the staff; and (4) fair treatment of all members of the staff by official leaders.

Communication

An important factor in any social structure is the free interchange of information, ideas, and opinions. Good communication is essential to instructional leadership involving the development of mutually desirable goals and means.

In even the best school situation there are examples of inadequate communication. These failures are often more conspicuous than instances of good communication, and they create much misunderstanding and anxiety. The concern teachers feel when they are uncertain of their teaching assignment or location for the following school year is an example of the damage inadequate communication can do. Programs of curriculum improvement frequently result in anxiety on the part of teachers because they do not know how the changes will affect them personally. Although the status leader who suggests re-examination of some aspect of the curriculum may have the greatest respect for his teachers, this respect may not be effectively communicated. Worry and apprehension are likely to result.

Even when concern about professional security is not involved, communication may greatly influence a staff member's feeling of being liked and accepted. The individual who knows that he is well informed about policy, program, and budget realizes that he, as an individual, is held to be important. His sense of involvement in the activities of the school and in the educational profession as a whole tends to increase. When staff members participate actively in making decisions, communication is, of course, greatly facilitated.

Effective communication is a two-way process, but it is

64

often difficult for teachers to communicate their ideas and reactions to official leaders. Even at the individual school level, unless clear channels of communication and a permissive atmosphere are developed, teachers' attitudes toward and ideas about many problems may never get through to official leaders. This means, inevitably, that status leaders are making judgments and forming opinions without information that is often crucial. Communication between teachers and central office personnel is an even more complicated process, and often there are no well-developed channels through which these groups can freely exchange beliefs and ideas.

The reasons for inadequate communication between official leaders and teachers are numerous and varied. Under the pressure of many daily details it is easy for status leaders to underestimate the importance of communication. Adequate communication takes time. Participation by teachers in the exploration and development of policy and program always contributes to more effective communication, but this also takes time. It may be necessary for instructional leaders to restudy and carefully revise the things they customarily do during a working day. Many serious interpersonal relations difficulties can be ameliorated if more attention is given to promoting the free interchange of ideas and opinions among all members of working groups.

Because of real or imagined dangers of misunderstanding, official leaders often screen carefully the information they give teachers. They seem to fear that certain items of information, if widely disseminated, may be misused by particular individuals. There may be differences of opinion within the administrative hierarchy as to what information should be made public. A principal, for example, may desire to discuss with his staff certain central office or board of education opinions or recommendations concerning instructional matters. If the director of instruction or the superintendent believes that this may lead to false rumors or unnecessary apprehension, the principal is faced with a difficult decision between loyalty and obedience to his superiors and action consistent with his convictions regarding the importance of free communication.

Official leaders may fail to communicate information for other reasons. Withholding information seems to increase the self-esteem of some individuals because they can use "private" information as a means of controlling others. In an insecure person secretiveness is a defensive reaction. He prefers to have his activities shrouded in mystery. Still another reason for withholding information is the tendency of some status leaders to underestimate the competence of staff members and the lay public. The conviction that others would either not understand or have nothing significant to contribute can be a real barrier to the dissemination of important information.

Teachers as well as status leaders may be inclined to withhold information. Staff members who feel that their opinions are not respected are not likely to attempt to communicate them. Many teachers, too, fear that the information they pass on to official leaders will be misused—will lead to reprisals against the person giving the information or against others implicated by it. There is a time-honored custom, in schools and many other organizations, of giving the official leader only the information it is believed he wants. As status leaders, we felt that we should be on guard against this barrier to adequate communication.

One of the principal difficulties in all communication is undoubtedly semantic. Many words do not have precise meanings. Even the term *curriculum* had some fifty different meanings as it was used in a sampling of professional literature. When there are added to this variety of "definitions" the highly personal meanings frequently attached to terms, the task of conveying information accurately through the use of words—especially written words—clearly becomes a difficult one.

Many school systems use various formal instruments for communicating information to staff groups. Newsletters or magazines are employed to disseminate information about school policy, specific practices in individual classrooms, events of interest, and other matters that may be of importance to teachers. In addition, instructional councils may be used to facilitate communication from staff members to official leaders. These councils often provide a desirable alternative to the usual, more formal, channels of communication.

It is our belief that (1) mutual goals-means leadership is dependent on good two-way communication between teachers and status leaders and (2) good communication can result only when there are many opportunities for free face-to-face discussion. Small group meetings provide such opportunities, and we found them especially effective in stimulating communication within individual schools. In general, conditions favorable to the frank expression of ideas and opinions can be created most easily at the individual school level. The principal or building curriculum coordinator is in a favorable position to understand the traditions, experiences, and reactions of those with whom he is associated, and this kind of understanding leads to better communication. The teaching group within a school often develops common attitudes toward the administration, toward work, toward in-service education, toward lay participation, toward students, and toward a variety of other important factors in the instructional situation. A building staff also tends to develop characteristic patterns of responding to administrative action, to orders and instructions, to problems faced by the group, to lay or professional criticism, and to many other specific situations. As the building status leader comes to recognize and understand these habitual attitudes

67

and patterns of behavior, he will be able to facilitate communication between his staff and other groups, such as central office personnel or parents in the school community.

There is an implication in these statements that the official leader who wishes to improve communication cannot rely on a simple, direct, factual presentation to achieve desired results. Feelings so influence the interpretation of facts that these, too, must be known and understood. An emotional response may be called forth by the facts themselves, by the person furnishing them, or by both. Facts presented by two different people using the same written source often arouse diverse reactions. Unless the reasons for responses of one kind or another are known and understood and their consequences anticipated, attempts at effective communication may prove futile.

School Organization

In our study of the effect of situational factors on leadership we were impressed by the importance of two aspects of school organization: (1) the formal organization, which is usually obvious to all members of the staff, and (2) the informal organization, which is frequently overlooked.

Formal Organization

We made no attempt to be systematic or comprehensive in our discussion and study of the formal organization of schools and school systems. We were concerned primarily with its effect on instructional leadership that stresses the development of mutually desirable goals and means. In Chapter 2 we discussed some of the difficulties likely to arise whenever mutual goals-means leadership is in conflict with that expected of principals or building curriculum coordinators by their superiors. We wish to consider here at somewhat greater length what can be done when this situation exists. The degree of conflict may, of course, vary from one building to another within a school system, and it may have different effects on the particular individuals involved.

We came to the conclusion that a principal or building curriculum coordinator can do much to develop leadership based on cooperation in almost any school system. As long as there is no specific ban on cooperative problem solving, nor any open hostility toward it, there is no reason why this kind of leadership cannot be exercised in at least some areas of the instructional program. When limits must be established, one of the major responsibilities of the principal is to help staff members identify carefully those areas in which they have freedom to make decisions and differentiate them sharply from those areas in which they do not have this freedom. The areas in which cooperative decision making at the individual school level is possible will vary from system to system. Decisions about teachers' social activities can almost always be made by individual staff groups. Individual schools are likely, in addition, to have a great deal of freedom in respect to the extraclass aspects of the curriculum, including all student activities and assemblies. In most school systems the teaching procedures actually used within individual classrooms can also be worked out cooperatively.

As we studied ourselves and our associates, we came to believe that much of the difficulty in developing the kind of instructional leadership we wanted to exercise resulted from a failure to make clear to members of a working group the limits within which they were free to make decisions and take action. Sometimes, of course, there is resistance to the idea of having to observe any restrictions. This is an unusual attitude, however, and rarely persists if there is free discussion of the whole question of limits. Laws, statutes, board of education rulings, well-established customs—all impose restraints on the freedom of choice of particular educational groups. It should be emphasized, however, that

69

attention to limits must come early in the problem solving process. Otherwise, decisions and actions are repudiated by persons outside the working group who must enforce whatever restrictions exist. This kind of repudiation leads to frustration, to disappointment, and to loss of confidence in cooperative work.

Informal Organization

By *informal organization* we mean simply the relationships that result from the natural tendency of people to associate with one another and to behave in accordance with the values of the small, informal groups to which they belong or desire to belong.

In some schools a closely knit and aggressive group of teachers can force the entire staff to take certain actions desired by only a small minority. This informal pressure group quite often does most of its work outside regular staff meetings, where decisions are supposed to be made. Although not all informal groups operate as directly or forcefully as this, they exist in most schools. Sometimes they are well-defined and recognizable cliques. At other times their existence is not known to official leaders or to many staff members.

Often the basis of organization of these informal groups is not clearly discernible and may, in fact, change from time to time; but sometimes, as with ethnic or religious groups, the reasons for membership are clear. Sometimes informal groups based on seniority or age serve to unite the old guard on a faculty. Single women may find it congenial to associate with one another, as may married women. A variety of other personal factors, such as manner of dress, physical appearance, or college background, may play a part in the formation of informal groups. Some may result directly from work on school problems and situations. For example, teams of people formed to develop a new aspect

70

of an instructional program, or individuals located in a particular wing of a building, or members of a single department may develop a pattern of intimate association and understanding. Temporary informal groups may result from rivalry among departments in a school or from the desire to support a particular candidate for a department chairmanship or principalship. Informal groups may be based on out-of-school social interests as well as professional interests.

Informal groups vary greatly in the control they exert over members, but almost all try to influence members to behave in accordance with group expectations. Threats of punishment and actual punishment are often resorted to. Punishment may take the form of ostracizing, or otherwise showing disapproval of, the nonconformist. New members of a staff are often "brought into line" by such methods.

Informal groups may have a desirable as well as an undesirable influence. Those that foster individual or group rivalry or tension are, of course, unhealthy. Groups that increase personal satisfactions, improve morale, or encourage cooperation are highly desirable.

As we have said, the reasons for the formation of specific informal groups are not always clear. It seemed to us, however, that the existence of many of them could be explained relatively simply. Ineffective official leadership sometimes results in the formation of informal groups to get done what the staff wants done. If the social needs of teachers are not being met, the formation of informal social groups is a natural result. Authoritarian leadership, providing little opportunity for participation in decision making, may tend to unify those who resist the directives of the person in authority.

Normally, informal groups have no membership lists, stated meeting times, or officers. When teachers seem to be well-organized against in-service education, or against change of any kind, or against overenthusiastic staff members, the actual structure of the group may not be discernible. Nevertheless, effective action may be taken against the individual who transgresses the group's code.

One important characteristic of informal organization is the unofficial leader, who is chosen by his group. He may, but usually does not, have any assigned leadership position. He always, however, is recognized by the group as being able and willing to provide means the group desires to use to achieve its purposes. Often this leader is an older person who has the respect of the group but lacks the characteristics essential to his becoming an official leader. Sometimes he is a young person who shows great promise for official leadership within the school hierarchy. Frequently he serves effectively as go-between for both teachers and administrators. Usually, when this kind of go-between is necessary, other, more desirable channels of communication are inadequate. As has been implied, unofficial leaders maintain their influence only as long as they seem to the group to be able to help determine or achieve goals the group considers desirable.

Our analysis of the informal organization of the schools with which we were associated revealed many ways in which this organization influenced the practices of the status leader. Each school staff appeared, at first, to be unique, but all the schools contained informal groups that influenced the behavior of their members. Although we were unable to devote much time to investigating the implications of this situation for leadership, we reached several tentative conclusions. We agreed that understanding the informal organization of a school helped to make clear some things that had previously been almost incomprehensible. Studying the various groups and the reasons for their formation helped us to understand the motivation of some staff members. We were frequently able to predict the position they would take on matters under consideration by the staff as a whole. We found, too, that if formal decisions did not have to be hurried, informal groups provided a good forum for discussion of problems and issues and served to facilitate communication and mutual understanding.

4

IMPROVEMENT OF
INSTRUCTIONAL LEADERSHIP

We believe that improving instructional leadership is one of the important problems faced by every city, county, and state school system. Yet leadership education has not received attention comparable to that given classroom supervision or course-of-study development. A growing body of evidence from fields other than education has increased our understanding of the process of improving instructional leadership. In connection with our work in Denver we encountered problems we believe other school systems are facing and developed ways of meeting these problems that may be applicable elsewhere. Consequently, we report in this chapter some of the things we learned about the leadership learning process and the environmental and psychological factors determining the effectiveness of a leadership education program. There is little likelihood that learning a set bundle of tricks or techniques will improve anyone's leadership. Successful leadership requires not only skills; it requires a great deal of insight and understanding.

Our conception of leadership implies that every member

74

of a group is likely to be seen at one time or another as a leader. That is, any individual in a group can at one time or another help others in the group, or all members of the group, in their efforts to clarify purposes and develop procedures useful in achieving these purposes. If the abilities of all its members are discovered and utilized, the group has a much wider range of talents and resources at its disposal than it would if it relied on those of only one—the official—leader. The effective dispersal of leadership functions requires, however, that groups take special pains to discover the abilities of their members and have some understanding of the kind of relationship between leaders and group members that results in the cooperative determination of goals and means.

Our belief that all members of a working group are under some circumstances recognized as leaders, or would be if their talents were known, led us to the conviction that a program of leadership education should involve staff members as well as status leaders. Training for group leadership can well be viewed as an integral part of in-service education. When leadership education projects are limited to status leaders, real difficulties are likely to arise. Leadership education may be viewed by those not involved in it as implying the somewhat secret and mysterious practice of techniques for manipulating others.

Learning to improve leadership implies working in situations in which human relations—the interactions among personalities—are exceedingly important. Whatever a principal may learn in order to reclassify the books on his shelves or the letters in his files does not usually require consideration of the judgment, feelings, or reactions of other people. Whenever he begins to experiment in order to improve his leadership, however, he is working with materials that, unlike books, react. If he studies the influence of frequent commendation on staff morale or the effect of cooperative

75

agenda planning on the productivity of staff committees, he is dealing with situations in which human relations are crucial. The effect of what he does is determined, in large part, by the interpretation the individuals with whom he works place on what he does.

Conditions Essential to an Effective Leadership Education Program

Before examining specific aspects of the process of leadership improvement, we would like to discuss some of the general conditions essential to the initiation and maintenance of an effective program of leadership education.

Compatibility of Goals and Means

The desirability of having leaders and those with whom they work seek mutual goals and mutually acceptable means applies, of course, to the establishment and development of a program of leadership education. The use of force, bargaining, or paternalism to get a leadership education program under way or to keep it going almost precludes developing an attitude that places high value on cooperative problem solving. The same kind of leadership it is hoped the participants in the program will learn should characterize the planning and carrying out of the program itself. When it does not—when the leaders of the program are not themselves committed to establishing its goals and the means of achieving these goals cooperatively—the program is not likely to succeed. The participants will actually experience a kind of leadership different from that which they are presumably learning to practice. And in many subtle as well as obvious ways they will be rewarded for conforming to this different conception of leadership. As a result, the kind of leadership exercised in the daily operation of the school system is much more likely to be learned.

76

If the cooperative development of goals and means has not been the usual method of getting the work of a school or a school system accomplished, it is to be expected that some of the participants in the program of leadership education will expect those who have initiated it to set the goals and describe the means of achieving them. There will inevitably be difficulties in overcoming this expectation. The program leaders, however, can help to do so by encouraging everyone—including, of course, themselves—to examine as objectively as possible his own leadership activities and the consequences of these activities.

Participation by Entire Official Leadership Hierarchy

Often it is assumed that leadership education can go on within any part of the official leadership hierarchy. We found that there were very real dangers in such an assumption. If principals, for example, are experimenting in order to improve their leadership and central office personnel are not, conceptions and practices incompatible with those of the leadership education program may manifest themselves in the operation of the school system. Similar conflicts are likely to arise if only one group of central office personnel— for example, the group responsible for instruction—participates in the leadership education program. As has been said, when the activities of the leadership education program, which occupy at most a day or so a month, are contradicted by the leadership practices rewarded during every working hour, the latter are much more likely to be learned. The behavior advocated in the leadership education program may even appear absurd when a quite different kind regularly results in recognition and promotion. Such discrepancies and conflicts occur unless the entire status leadership hierarchy within a school system at least understands and supports the leadership program. If all levels can be actively involved, so much the better.

It seemed to some of us that the higher the leader's status, as judged by salary or title, the less his disposition to experiment with new techniques in the area of interpersonal relations. There are probably a number of reasons for this. One is that the leader with high status may feel that he has too much at stake to experiment. Mistakes are relatively more costly—and more obvious—at higher levels of an administrative hierarchy than at lower levels. High-ranking status leaders may feel that a mistake resulting from planned experimentation is more to be feared than a mistake that just "happens" in the course of events.

We frequently sensed, too, that it seemed to be more difficult for a leader with high status to make the admission, implied by experimentation, that his current leadership practices are not as effective as they might be. This reluctance to admit limitations is reinforced by the attitude of his associates. Many of them would lose confidence in his leadership if he admitted his shortcomings very often. This he knows. The higher a person is in an administrative hierarchy, the more he is in the public eye, and the larger the group is that looks to him for guidance. Appearing uncertain about what should be done, in front of so many people—and planned experimentation implies uncertainty—is sometimes almost intolerable.

A final reason for the tendency of those with important administrative positions to experiment gingerly, if at all, with new techniques in the area of interpersonal relations is probably related to their age, experience, and success. Most persons are selected for high administrative positions because they have already demonstrated their ability to deal effectively with people and have shown a firm, if not dominating or autocratic, kind of leadership. This selection is often made by laymen, and it is influenced by the cultural stereotype of the strong leader—a person who knows what he wants and can get other people to do it with a minimum of friction. The value of more cooperative ways of working with people has been emphasized relatively recently; and this approach has undoubtedly had greater influence on the younger, less experienced men and women in a school system.

When all the status leaders within a school system cannot, for some reason, be actively involved in cooperative efforts to improve leadership, those not actively participating can encourage the program by letting it be known that they believe the effort is important and worth while. As with any in-service education activity, there is the constant danger that the leadership education program will be crowded out by the pressure of competing activities.

One tangible way of supporting a program of leadership education is to provide released time or to make some other adjustment of responsibilities. In the Denver project the most frequently reported barrier to experimentation was lack of time (see Chapter 8, p. 194). This was true in spite of the fact that Denver school policy encourages in-service education on school time and arrangements are made to implement this policy.

Even more important than released time, however, is the recognition of the program's value by top administrators. This recognition is essential if new practices are to be extended to the operation of the school system. If high-ranking administrators (1) encourage experimentation with new leadership techniques, (2) give tangible support when difficulties arise because of experimentation, and (3) encourage the widespread adoption of techniques proved to be effective, everyone participating in the program will be more likely to regard it as important. In our leadership education activities we were greatly encouraged and supported whenever it was possible for the superintendent and assistant superintendent in charge of secondary schools to meet with us. This happened frequently.

Adequate Preparation

The importance of assuring understanding of what a leadership education program involves and the necessity of arousing real desire to participate *before* the program is initiated cannot be overemphasized. There is real danger that recruitment efforts will be brief and entirely verbal. Some status leaders find it easy to say, "Yes, we want to improve. A leadership education program sounds good." This ready assent may be based, however, on inadequate understanding of what is involved. If a serious program is launched—one that requires actually trying out and evaluating new and presumably better leadership practices—criticism mounts. Many persons say later that they had no idea of the amount of work the project would entail.

It is therefore important, before any program is formally initiated, to elicit the ideas prospective participants may have regarding desirable activities, problems likely to arise, and possible starting points. Although this kind of discussion is necessary, it is not sufficient. Actual demonstration of what are considered, at the time, to be promising activities, followed by discussion and evaluation, helps to create realistic expectations. Obtaining from prospective participants carefully considered reactions to all proposals assures a better understanding of what the program can accomplish and how it will operate.

If the leadership education program uses as a starting point problems brought up for consideration by participants, discussion clarifying various conceptions of leadership and analyzing the relation of specific practices employed by participants to these conceptions is helpful. It should be kept in mind, however, that at the beginning, the leadership problems people are willing to talk about in a group situation are likely to be the "respectable" rather than the real problems.

Atmosphere of Freedom

A non-threatening atmosphere, which encourages participation by all the people involved in the leadership education project, is important for several reasons. New patterns of action and relationship are frequently resisted because they involve threats to personal security. A free and flexible psychological climate allows "space" for individual struggle and growth. A permissive working situation also provides the leaders of the program with excellent opportunities for becoming familiar with the perceptions of the individuals involved, and vice versa.

An atmosphere of freedom is necessary, too, for frank and penetrating self-evaluation. We found that critical self-examination helped to disturb our complacency about our relations with other people, encouraged us to examine more objectively the quality of human relations in situations in which we exercised leadership functions, and provided a basis for assessing progress.

Our willingness to try out more promising leadership practices and generalize from the consequences depended to a large extent on our personal security. When we felt threatened for any of a variety of reasons, we were generally reluctant to try out new ideas. The common reaction to threat was aggression or withdrawal. Freedom from threat is not, of course, prerequisite only to improving leadership. It is probably fundamental to all learning. We are convinced, however, that friendly and permissive relations among all persons involved in a leadership education program not only encourage experimentation but are essential to it.

Opportunities for Group Work

In a group situation it is possible not only to observe a variety of leadership roles and practices but to obtain some evaluation of them. It is in a group situation that changes

81

in behavior are most likely to be brought about. Group decision and action foster modification in both ideology and habit. A substantial part of the Denver leadership project involved group work, in which there was an opportunity to study at first hand many of the important human relations factors in leadership and to profit from the support of others when experimentation was undertaken. Leadership education appears to be most effective when it provides for situations in which more desirable behavior can be learned through participation, practice, and group evaluation.

Emphasis on the importance of group work as part of a leadership education program does not mean that instructional leadership is limited to face-to-face group situations. Helping individual teachers with instructional problems, counseling with them on personal or professional matters, and otherwise assisting individual professional workers or lay citizens interested in instruction—all require improved skills and understandings. A comprehensive leadership education program should devote attention to these as well as to leadership procedures appropriate for group situations.

The Leadership Learning Process

As we discussed and clarified our ideas about leadership and began to try out new leadership practices, we realized that leadership improvement was a complicated learning process. The following aspects of this learning process were eventually differentiated out of the total complex of our activities:

1. Dissatisfaction with present leadership practices

2. Identification of what seem to be more desirable practices

3. Formulation of hypotheses—that is, predicting that certain desirable goals will be achieved if specific actions are taken

4. Testing of hypotheses in action
5. Collection and analysis of evidence concerning the consequences of these actions, on which subsequent generalizations can then be based

Each of these aspects will be commented on in the sections that follow. The five do not, of course, represent a fixed sequence of discrete steps. However, it should be emphasized that improvement in leadership—especially the possibility of continuing to improve one's leadership—requires attention to each of these aspects of the leadership learning process and the development of understandings and skills appropriate to each.

Dissatisfaction with Present Leadership Practices

A feeling that present practices are not satisfactory is basic to the attempt of any individual to improve his leadership. Until he is dissatisfied with what he is doing, he is not likely to make much effort to change. This does not imply that all persons who may volunteer to participate in a leadership education program are very deeply disturbed about their behavior. As we have said, it is not difficult to accumulate a relatively large group of "volunteers" for leadership study or improvement.

The strongest motivation for change comes from a person's dissatisfaction with his own behavior, not from the realization that other people are displeased at what he does. The latter realization can undoubtedly motivate change in some circumstances, but the change is then directed toward pleasing other people rather than improving leadership. These two purposes are frequently at variance. We found it important, in connection with our attempts to improve leadership, to differentiate between dissatisfaction that results from self-scrutiny and that which results from the censure and criticism of others. Censure is likely to be threatening and to lead to self-defense or psychological withdrawal. As we have already said, neither defense nor withdrawal is conducive to improvement.

In the Denver project there were great individual differences in dissatisfaction—in the gap between the kind of leadership we wanted to practice and that which we felt we were practicing. Within any group of educational leaders there will be some who are clearly dissatisfied with their leadership and others who are generally satisfied with what they are able to do.

During the course of the project we accumulated some relatively objective evidence concerning differences in dissatisfaction with self, so far as human relations beliefs and practices were concerned. We adapted to our needs an inventory entitled "Ideas about Myself," which had first been used by the 1950 National Training Laboratory in Group Development. Some of the forty-five statements included in this inventory were the following: "I think I have a pretty clear understanding of how the people I work with see themselves and the job they are trying to do. . . . It is important to me to maintain my individuality within any group to which I belong. . . . I often get so involved in doing a particular job that I don't pay much attention to the feelings and reactions of other people concerned. . . . My first reaction to a proposal that things be done differently is usually negative." [1]

We reacted to these statements twice. The first reaction indicated the extent to which we believed the statement to be descriptive of our present attitude and behavior. The second reaction indicated the extent to which we would have liked the statement to be descriptive of us. This second reaction revealed our aspirations so far as the interpersonal relations aspect of leadership was concerned. By counting the number of items to which each person had reacted in such a way as to indicate dissatisfaction with present be-

[1] The inventory is reproduced in its entirety in the Appendix, p. 202–204.

havior, we were able to obtain some measure of differences in the degree of dissatisfaction felt by individual group members. The range in degree of dissatisfaction, thus defined, was from 1 to 25, with a median of 7. One individual, in other words, expressed a desire for substantial change in behavior in his reaction to only one of the forty-five items. Another person expressed such a desire in his reaction to twenty-five of the forty-five items.

A considerable amount of self-examination followed the use of the inventory just described. Some of it was superficial and contributed little to either understanding of weaknesses or desire to change. But discussion among small groups of people who felt comfortable enough with one another to admit their limitations freely helped to identify areas of inadequacy and led to stronger inclination to change. As we have said, self-examination in a group situation is limited by the psychological atmosphere the group has developed. We found that the larger the group, the greater the status differences among its members, and the greater the number of insecure individuals in it, the less fruitful self-examination and group discussion tended to be.

We had some success in developing dissatisfaction through reading and discussion of the literature about leadership. The discussions, of course, made extensive use of our personal experience as status leaders. Although talk about instructional leadership heightened our sensitivity to what we were doing and increased the dissatisfaction of some people, the chief gain probably was in our ability to *talk* about better leadership. Talk alone did not, however, affect very noticeably our willingness to experiment.

Analyzing the reactions of participants to a situation in which leadership had been exercised was another procedure that helped us to see weaknesses in our present leadership practices. To obtain these reactions, we usually employed some kind of post-meeting evaluation questionnaire, which asked group members to rate the effectiveness of the meeting and explain briefly the reasons for their rating. Explanations frequently called attention to the way the person or persons who had served as leaders had acted. As members of the group became more analytical in their thinking about leadership and group behavior, their observations and suggestions became more pointed and specific. Usually the post-meeting evaluations were not signed. In groups whose members had developed a relationship that made them feel reasonably safe in expressing and accepting suggestions and criticism, however, anonymity was considered to be less important.

Obtaining post-meeting reactions is one way of trying to determine somewhat objectively the consequences of specific leadership practices. In subsequent group discussions these consequences can be compared with expectations. Because it makes possible a more precise determination of whether or not a specific practice leads to the consequences anticipated, this kind of comparison seems to us to be one of the best methods of increasing willingness to change. Most of our previous attempts to find out whether or not our actions achieved the desired results had been relatively unsystematic and subjective.

A final procedure we found useful in increasing our sensitivity to our limitations as leaders involved observation and discussion of role-playing situations. The situations were usually designed in such a way as to enable two or three persons independently to practice leadership of one kind or another in a specific simulated situation. A role-player might exercise the kind of leadership he himself considered most effective, or he might choose to imitate the behavior of another person with leadership responsibilities. Frequently, after a role-playing episode demonstrating unsuccessful leadership had been concluded, group members commented that for the first time they had seen themselves as they must often appear to others. Watching two different people role-play a chairman—one demonstrating behavior that obstructs group work, the other, behavior that expedites it—caused most of us to examine more carefully the way we acted in analogous circumstances. Undoubtedly we failed, in many instances, to see ourselves in the undesirable role. Others might say privately or publicly that that was the way we behaved, but the ability to see ourselves as others saw us came slowly and with difficulty.

Identification of More Desirable Practices

Dissatisfaction with our present instructional leadership did not necessarily mean that we had very clear ideas about what we might do that would be better. We found, in fact, that it frequently led to feelings of frustration. Frustration had some wholesome consequences, however. We began to work more intensively in two problem areas and, as a result, eventually developed a clearer understanding of how we might increase the effectiveness of our leadership. First, we spent a great deal of time clarifying ideas about the kind of instructional leadership we wanted to exercise. Second, we gradually learned the importance of defining more explicitly the particular instructional problems on which individuals or groups were working. This, when done cooperatively by all the persons involved, made our goals clearer and helped us determine ways and means of achieving them. Just what might be done to fulfill the function of leadership—to provide individuals or groups with help in the cooperative identification of their goals and the means of achieving them—then became more explicit.

Clarifying ideas about instructional leadership. The Denver group worked hard and long to develop its conception of the nature of leadership. Early in the project this matter came up for consideration again and again. Even after the emphasis had shifted to practice, considerable satisfaction continued to be expressed about meetings in which the nature of leadership had been discussed.

In the early stages of our work we gave considerable attention to (1) the role of the leader and the nature of leadership; (2) the persons who might function as instructional leaders; and (3) the scope of our concern with leadership. We considered whether the leader's function is to set goals, define policy, and secure group approval and acceptance or to provide what assistance he can to the group as it defines its goals and determines means of achieving them. A series of related questions asked whether leadership is a matter of exhibiting certain traits—such as courage, firmness, and insight—or a matter of adapting to varying conditions and situations. Some of the questions concerned the persons who might function as leaders—were the status leaders in our group the only possible leaders, or might classroom teachers be the leaders at times? We discussed whether leaders are born or made—whether or not one can learn to lead, whether or not one can increase his leadership skill.

Our definition of *leadership* and some of the implications of this definition have already been discussed. We want here to do no more than call attention briefly to some of the important incidental benefits resulting from our consideration of the nature of leadership. First, most of us found that although we had been holding status leadership positions for a long time, we had not tried very diligently to clarify our conception of our task. We were too busy with things that had to be done—keeping our desks clear and meeting our calendar of appointments. Although the progress we made in these discussions seemed at times to be slow, most of us came to appreciate the importance of thinking about our work as well as doing it.

Second, our ability to communicate with one another improved. At first, although we often used the same words, our meanings were different. The expression *democratic leadership,* for example, had various connotations. As we clarified our own ideas about instructional leadership, we found that we were more successful in talking with staff groups about what we were doing in the leadership project. These conversations with our associates helped us to realize that the kind of leadership we were able to exercise was a consequence not only of how we felt but also of the way the people with whom we were working felt. The teachers often had ideas about effective instructional leadership that seemed to be in conflict with our own.

Third, our discussions of the nature of leadership helped us to see more clearly the great disparity between what we felt we ought to be doing and what we actually were doing. Trying to understand the reasons for this disparity brought to our attention some of the difficulties we would face in implementing our ideas. At first we were probably optimistic about the effect clarification of concepts would have on behavior. We were inclined to believe that as our understanding increased, our practices would improve. Certainly this was true, but to a limited degree only. As has been said before, there is a great difference between being able to discuss leadership intelligently and engaging in intelligent leadership. Some of the data presented in Chapter 8 suggest that, on the whole, we tended to be realistic in our expectation of how significantly talk would modify practice. From the beginning of the project we were better satisfied with our ideas about leadership than with our leadership behavior. We exhibited different degrees of impatience with discussion alone and devoted a great deal of attention, throughout the project, to the testing of presumably better practices.

Finally, a fact that became clearer as we considered the nature of leadership was that our ideas about leadership often had their roots in preconceptions about the people we worked with. When we had confidence in our associates and their ability to work effectively on problems they were concerned about, we found it easier to behave in a way that was consistent with our ideas about cooperative curriculum improvement. When we did not have this confidence in our associates and their ability, we found the gap between our professions and practices a wide one.

Experimenting with leadership practices. Our definition of *leadership* did not make explicit many of the specific practices that would have to be learned if we were to become better instructional leaders. We devoted a great deal of time and thought, however, to experimenting with procedures that might help groups identify problems and determine methods of solving these problems. This, of course, led us to a consideration of group process; and one of the first subgroups established concentrated on trying to learn more about group dynamics. Interest was practical rather than theoretical and led to the identification of the various functions that must be fulfilled by someone in the group if work is to be expedited. Members of this subgroup were helped by the analysis Benne and Sheats[2] had made of the functional roles of group members. The roles of chairman, recorder, and process observer were rotated among members of the group, and each person's actions were carefully evaluated.

In the total group meetings, too, at least incidental attention was always given to our methods of working. As has been said, written post-meeting reactions were obtained regularly, and we tried to use the data obtained to improve future meetings. Throughout the project some of us were skeptical about the emphasis placed on group process. Several times the mistake was made of considering ways of working as if they had intrinsic value, and when this happened, some members of the group lost interest. We made most progress in our study of process when we realized we had to give it attention in order to accomplish our work.

[2] Kenneth Benne and Paul Sheats, "Functional Roles of Group Members," *Journal of Social Issues,* 4:42–47, Spring 1948.

Even then we often found that the use of technical group dynamics terminology was as likely to impede communication as to facilitate it.

The evaluation data presented in Chapter 8 indicate that, in spite of occasional dissatisfaction on the part of some of the participants, those learnings related to methods of working in groups were considered to be the most valuable learnings resulting from the project. The point requiring emphasis is that we wanted, as a total group, to learn whatever we had to learn about process *in order to get on with the job*. A few of us, however, became sufficiently interested in the interactions of group members to make a special study of the factors involved.

Before concluding this section, we would like to comment on the importance of trying to identify, as clearly as possible, whatever obstacles there may be to the achievement of a particular goal by a specific group. The more explicitly these obstacles can be identified, the more easily they can be surmounted or circumvented.

One of the Denver experiments designed to increase the participation of parents in curriculum planning illustrates clearly the importance of identifying specific obstacles. The conventional large PTA assembly made it so difficult for parents to express themselves that very few of them participated actively. When attempts were made to divide the total group into smaller discussion and study groups, the results were not encouraging. An analysis of the situation indicated that inadequate leading of discussion in these small groups was the major obstacle to their success. When a training program for discussion group leadership was initiated, the productivity of the small PTA groups increased appreciably.

Formulation of Hypotheses

Ordinarily, after dissatisfaction with present leadership practices had developed among a group of Denver status leaders and more promising practices had been identified, an action hypothesis was formulated. That is, it was predicted that if a specific action were taken, certain desirable results would be achieved.

For example, one principal and curriculum coordinator were concerned about staff morale in their school. After some reading, study, and discussion, they concluded tentatively that they might not have been sufficiently responsive to group wishes. They decided to try to improve morale by helping the teachers identify and work on school problems of real concern to them. They proceeded to test the following hypothesis: *If we help teachers to identify and work on their problems, morale will be improved.*

Another curriculum coordinator decided, on the basis of informal conversations with teachers, that they were facing many instructional problems to which the professional literature gave considerable attention. She believed that if teachers became aware of pertinent sources in the literature and used them, they would be able to deal with their problems more effectively. She proceeded to test this hypothesis: *If it is made easier and more pleasant for teachers to read professional literature that brings new problems to their attention and deals with instructional problems they have already identified, they will be better able to handle these problems and will express satisfaction with the help they are receiving.*

In another school there was considerable dissatisfaction with the relation of guidance to the curriculum. Procedures for integrating guidance with the total school program were therefore sought. As a result of reading and study, the principal and curriculum coordinator concluded that if the teachers themselves identified guidance problems and cooperatively planned ways of dealing with these problems, the desired integration would be brought about. They then tested this hypothesis: *If teachers identify guidance prob-*

92

lems and cooperatively attempt to solve these problems, guidance will tend to be integrated with the total school program.

The quality of hypothesizing varied from situation to situation, and at least three factors were involved in improvement. One was willingness to listen to or read about what other people had tried and found successful when facing similar problems. Another was the ability to examine our own past experience critically. Most of us, however, were more skillful at critical reading than at critical examination of our own experience. The third factor was the ability to formulate hypotheses that could be tested. Many of our hypotheses were at first far too general. Little information was given about either the actions proposed or the consequences anticipated. As we acquired more experience with action research, we learned to describe more explicitly what we planned to do and what we hoped would happen as a result.

Testing Hypotheses in Action

An essential feature of any leadership education program is the provision that is made for trying out the practices that seem to be more promising than those previously engaged in. The worth of leadership education cannot be measured by improvement in the way a leader talks about what he has done or is going to do. It must be measured by the changes in his behavior and by the consequences of these changes.

The extent to which we felt free to try out new and more promising leadership practices varied greatly from individual to individual and from situation to situation. We have already said that experimentation was not likely to take place when we felt under pressure or threatened in any way. Frequently we all considered some procedure promising and supported it with many strong arguments. But, given a particular meeting, we could not bring ourselves to try it out. We had this difficulty a number of times in connection with obtaining post-meeting reactions. Although we were convinced that this method of evaluating meetings would help the leader as well as the group and that requesting the reactions was reasonable, we nevertheless were unwilling to do so. This unwillingness was most noticeable when we thought that the people attending a meeting were there, not because of a deep conviction that something would be done about a matter that concerned them, but because they had been asked to attend or felt they had to. Since we were verbally committed to voluntary participation in meetings and cooperative planning of agenda, we felt insecure whenever these conditions had been violated. This insecurity undoubtedly explains in part our reluctance to obtain post-meeting reactions. Some of us probably suspected what the reactions would be and were not certain whether we would be able to improve the situation.

What this means is that our ability and willingness to experiment with more promising practices in the leadership education project itself gave no assurance that we would apply what we had learned or experiment with analogous practices in our daily work. The setting of the leadership project was favorable to experimentation. The psychological atmosphere encouraged it. We often hesitated, however, to try out new practices in situations in which everyone was seriously at work on an actual instructional problem. These situations were, we felt, crucial, and we tended to do what we had always done because we knew we could do it. Although the consequences might not be all that we desired, the old pattern of behavior was at least familiar. We hesitated to try out new and presumably better practices under actual working conditions because we were not confident we could do so successfully.

Another obstacle to trying out new practices was the

94

time and energy involved. We all carried a normal load of responsibilities, and the period of the project was especially strenuous because of a number of attacks on the public schools by certain lay groups. Although we might hypothesize that a specific change in our behavior, such as preliminary agenda planning by a group, would have desirable results, the fact that the change involved additional time and energy acted as a deterrent. The difficulty of finding the minutes necessary to canvass a group for agenda suggestions sometimes prevented our taking even the initial step. And the testing of such a hypothesis often involved new problems—determining what kind of data we could obtain that would help us ascertain the effectiveness of the new practice, obtaining the data, and interpreting them. Because of either a lack of time or a lack of interest, we found that we might discontinue the action research process at any one of these points. Sometimes the other people involved in our projects seemed unable to find time to provide us with the information we needed. Sometimes we obtained the data but did not have time to interpret and use them.

We tested a number of hypotheses in role-playing situations. We tried to make the role-playing as realistic as possible, and we found that it helped many of us to try out new leadership practices, analyze the consequences, and formulate generalizations. We did not, however, engage in a great deal of role-playing. Post-meeting reactions obtained immediately after this kind of training session usually indicated great satisfaction. However, probably because we did not follow up systematically what we had learned, and because role-playing was used relatively infrequently, the over-all reaction to this method of practicing leadership skills was not very favorable. In evaluating the various activities in which we had engaged during the leadership project, we ranked role-playing fifteenth on a list of seventeen (see Chapter 8, p. 174).

Collection and Analysis of Evidence Concerning Consequences

As we have said several times, we tried throughout our experimentation and study and practice to use an action research approach. Although we frequently found it difficult to devise ways of getting satisfactory evidence concerning the effects of new leadership practices, we were usually able, by giving thought to the matter, to obtain better evidence than we had been able to obtain before. The more carefully we thought about evidence, however, the more dissatisfied we became with the usual methods of obtaining it.

We often had serious difficulties in interpreting the data we collected. Frequently we were not at all certain what generalizations they supported. If they seemed to buttress some of our cherished beliefs, we were likely to welcome them with enthusiasm. When predictions growing out of deep convictions were not supported, we found it easy to criticize the design of the experiment and the data resulting from it. It was necessary to guard constantly against using selected data for illustrative purposes and to discipline ourselves to use whatever data we obtained as a basis for inference only. But, in spite of these difficulties, we developed an increased awareness of the importance of evidence— of the importance of facts.

Learning Experiences Contributing to Leadership Improvement

The wishes and attitudes of participants are crucial in deciding the suitability of various learning experiences for a program of leadership education. They determine the acceptability of any particular learning experience and, consequently, the degree of involvement of specific individuals. Some members of the Denver group never found particularly worth while several of the activities in which the group as a whole decided to engage. As a result, a few discontinued their participation in the project. Others, although continuing to meet with the group, did so without real interest or involvement.

The extent to which individuals desired or were able to change their behavior in part determined what activities they found worth while. As we have said, some members of the group were much less satisfied with their leadership than others. Some who expressed considerable dissatisfaction found it difficult to experiment with new procedures. The attitude of individuals toward group activities was strongly influenced also by the way their participation in the project had been secured, by the results they expected from it, and by the attitude of other members of the group. Early in the project the interest of several participants lessened when reports they gave about work they were doing with a great deal of enthusiasm were received by the total group with apathy. This situation calls attention again to the importance of group support for the kind of experimentation in which we engaged.

An effective leadership education program must eventually modify the perceptions, aspirations, insights, understandings, attitudes, and skills of actual and potential leaders. If this comprehensive learning is to take place, a wide variety of learning experiences must be provided. Learning experiences that make possible new aspirations are often different from those leading to the development of skills. And because an isolated learning experience does not result in a change in understanding or attitude or skill, the sequence of experiences must be planned to accomplish most effectively the specific purposes sought.

Another important factor in the selection of activities is

97

the readiness of the group to benefit from a particular experience at a given time. The Denver leadership project followed no over-all training plan. Goals and means of achieving them were developed as we progressed. We felt that this was a psychologically sound procedure, and the one holding the greatest promise for stimulating self-direction and initiative.

In the sections that follow, the various kinds of learning experiences we found fruitful are commented on, and the learnings to which each made a particularly important contribution are noted.

Reading, Discussion, and Analysis

Our attitudes, values, and understandings relative to leadership were, of course, a consequence of our previous experience. Any modification that took place occurred as a result of new experiences or because past experiences were re-examined and re-interpreted. Explanation, analysis, and interpretation of specific leadership practices helped us in this kind of learning. Verbalization is probably essential if important distinctions among various conceptions of leadership are to be raised to the level of consciousness. Only then can they be examined and more adequate conceptions developed.

At times our learning experiences had to be viewed in relation to the objectives and philosophy of our particular school or the entire school system and in relation to our functions within the school or system. A program of leadership education must take into account the official duties and responsibilities pertaining to particular leadership positions. An awareness of assigned responsibilities assisted us materially in both the selection and development of training experiences. In the analysis of job functions and school policies, activities that were primarily verbal—lectures, discussions, reading, and conferences—again helped greatly.

Group Decision and Action

The role played by group decision and action in changing individual attitudes and behavior has been referred to several times, but because of its importance it is emphasized again here. The effectiveness of exclusively verbal approaches, such as lectures or group discussions, is limited not only because the words used often fail to make meanings clear but because resulting improvement is primarily in talking about leadership rather than exercising it. The contribution lectures and discussions can make when they are combined with group decision and action, however, is significant.

Realistic Learning Situations

Reference has already been made to the value of planned demonstration through role-playing or sociodrama and to the desirability of utilizing, for illustration and analysis, the day-to-day experiences of members of the group. Probably the most important function of a realistic learning situation is to make concrete and vivid the various leadership practices and group procedures that may be employed to achieve specific purposes. We were usually able to transfer what we had learned to our work more easily when we had actually observed certain practices than when these had been merely described.

Individual Testing and Practice

Perhaps the most important part of a leadership education program is actual practice of learnings. Information about leadership techniques or skills is not sufficient. Situations must actually be diagnosed and skills and understandings applied in action. As we have implied many times, the practice of learnings may take many forms. Role-playing has already been mentioned. On-the-job experimentation

99

is another form of practice, one in which there is opportunity to try things out in real situations, preferably under supervision so that another person can help with analysis and evaluation. The supervision we received in connection with on-the-job experimentation was not systematic or continuous, but we did our best to help one another. In addition, a kind of research supervision was provided by the Institute consultants.

We concluded that individual testing and practice was probably the most effective method of improving leadership, although the support we gave one another in the group situation was essential to our willingness and ability to experiment alone. This emphasis on individual activity to some extent limited the range of experiences any one person encountered. However, our ability to generalize from what happened in specific situations increased as our work continued and made the wider application of learnings possible.

Many leadership techniques or skills may have to be practiced. Skills involved in self-analysis, in recruiting interest and stimulating activity, in diagnosing problems, in assessing perceptions, in improving group discussion, in evaluating leadership, in conducting action research—all are important and may require considerable practice before they are learned and can be effectively applied.

Part Two THE DENVER LEADERSHIP PROJECT

5

THE DENVER SETTING

Denver in 1950 had a population of about 400,000. Its current rate of growth is substantially above the national average. The school district, which is conterminous with the city and county, includes seventy elementary schools, eleven junior high schools, five senior high schools, and the Emily Griffith Opportunity School, an adult vocational and self-improvement institution. These schools are attended by approximately 55,000 boys and girls and 25,000 adults. Nearly 2,200 teachers are employed in the system.

The Denver public schools are organized on the 6–3–3 basis, although there are a few exceptions because of geographic or building-size factors. The persons with major status leadership responsibilities in each of the junior and senior high schools are the principal, the assistant principal, the dean, and the coordinator of instruction. The principal is thought of as the instructional leader of his school. A great deal of freedom is given him and his faculty to develop and carry out instructional activities within the framework established by city-wide committees on instruction.[1]

[1] For a more complete description of the organization of these committees see Hollis L. Caswell and associates, *Curriculum Improvement in Public School Systems* (New York, Bureau of Publications, Teachers College, Columbia University, 1950), chap. vii.

For many years the principal had been expected not only to serve as the instructional leader of his school but to take care of all the other pressing and time-consuming duties that make a principal's life so harried. In order to lighten his load, official approval was given in the spring of 1949 to the appointment of instructional coordinators in each of the secondary schools. These coordinators, under the direction of their principals, were given responsibility for the maintenance and improvement of the instructional program.

In each school the initial appointee to the position of coordinator of instruction had been a member of the faculty of that school. Although this kind of appointment has certain advantages, difficulties frequently arise when a faculty member is appointed to a position in the same school that carries with it increased status and salary. The difficulties become more complex when, as in Denver, the position is a newly created one and considerable faculty doubt exists concerning its desirability.

As has been said, throughout the history of the Denver schools the supervision of instruction in individual secondary schools had been primarily the responsibility of principals. All of them recognized that the press of other duties did not permit them to do this job adequately. Nevertheless, there was great uncertainty about how much authority should be delegated to the coordinators. There was uncertainty, too, about how to help faculties accept the new appointees. It seemed reasonable to assume that part of the problem connected with the newly appointed coordinators would be the development of an effective team to do a job one person had attempted to do before on a part-time basis. In addition, certain changes in the working relationship of central office supervisory personnel and the personnel of the individual schools were necessitated by the appointment of instructional coordinators. Previously, all supervisory matters had been channeled through the principal's office. It became apparent that many supervisory details would now be handled by the coordinators.

In view of the novelty of the work that the Denver secondary school instructional coordinators were trying to do, and because of the serious problems they were facing, the Denver schools in March, 1949, invited the Horace Mann-Lincoln Institute of School Experimentation to assist them in a study of effective instructional leadership. Because the principal and the coordinator constituted an instructional leadership team in each secondary school, the principals also were included in the study.

Denver Curriculum Improvement Policy

Since 1922 the Denver schools have been committed to the belief that the persons most deeply involved in a problem are the ones who should participate in its solution. The initial step in implementing this belief was the adoption of a plan to grant teachers released time to prepare courses of study and related learning materials. Although the nature of the projects has varied through the years, the policy of teacher responsibility for the determination of educational objectives and the development of teaching techniques has continued.

The use of consultants in the solution of school problems has an even longer history, dating back to the Denver Survey of 1917. Since that time the services of scores of outstanding educational leaders have been utilized in the improvement of the Denver schools. In addition, the schools have welcomed the opportunity to participate in studies of national scope. During the past twenty-five years Denver has been included in the Eight Year Study of the Relationship between School and College, the Stanford Social Studies Investigation, the Cooperative Study of Teacher Education

105

of the American Council on Education, the Intergroup Education in Cooperating Schools Project, and several studies of the Horace Mann-Lincoln Institute of School Experimentation.

At least two interesting facts should be mentioned in connection with all these studies. The first is that in each case the pattern of participation was in harmony with the belief that those involved in and affected by a problem should participate in its solution. The second is that in no study did participation involve cooperative action *among* schools. The uniqueness of each school community was recognized and emphasized, and each was encouraged to work as a unit. This method of operating has distinct advantages, but it does not always make for system-wide solidarity or the rapid testing in all schools of what has been found desirable in a few.

In the Denver schools, supervision is viewed as an aspect of curriculum improvement. The kind of supervision that is synonymous with inspection has almost completely disappeared. The assumption is that improved teaching and learning will result from the cooperative solution of instructional problems. Improvement in instructional leadership, therefore, was viewed as requiring increased skill in defining and solving problems, keener awareness of the factors involved in this process, and better understanding of human relations.

The Leadership Project

As has been said, the Horace Mann-Lincoln Institute was not new to Denver. Several previous studies had been undertaken in cooperation with individual school faculties and smaller groups of teachers. At the time the leadership project was initiated, the Institute was planning to concentrate most of its research on secondary school problems. The desirability of an investigation of instructional leadership at that level was immediately recognized.

Staff members of the Horace Mann-Lincoln Institute work with associated school systems in a way that is consistent with Denver curriculum improvement policy. Committed to action research, which assumes that social problems are a function of the situation in which they arise, Institute consultants had already helped Denver school personnel to apply action research techniques to the solution of their problems. The two Institute consultants who participated in the leadership project had the additional advantages of deep interest in the improvement of instructional leadership and previous acquaintance with the Denver schools.

Working together, the principals and coordinators of the Denver secondary schools, a limited number of Denver central office personnel, and the consultants from the Horace Mann-Lincoln Institute tackled the problem of improving the quality of instructional leadership. The study was the first one undertaken in Denver on so broad a base. In previous years attempts to spread throughout the system the results obtained from pilot-school experiments had met with little success. It is often assumed that if pilot groups have been selected by the total group, and if they keep the total group informed, all will move ahead together. This had not happened in Denver. Consequently, it was thought that by involving the total group of secondary school principals and coordinators from the beginning, widespread dissemination of findings and modification of practices would be assured.

Meetings of the total group were held in the spring of 1949, and an exploration of instructional leadership problems and possible ways of working was begun. It soon became apparent that forty people could not work very effectively without developing some acceptable basis for dividing into smaller groups. During that spring the problems raised by the total group seemed to relate to three broad areas: (1) leadership in in-service education, (2) group process, and (3) specific leadership procedures. Three subgroups, corresponding to the three problem areas, were formed, each person choosing the group whose work interested him most. Although the participants set to work with a will, certain difficulties soon became apparent. Since there were three subgroups and only two Institute consultants, one group was left without a consultant, or at least its members felt that it was. Because of differences in the problems under investigation, the subgroups were at widely varying distances from achievement of their goals. Variations in the approaches used by the three subgroups tended to reduce the effectiveness of communication among them. Because the proportion of principals, coordinators, and central office personnel varied from one group to another, the subgroups tended to draw apart on a status basis. Differences in the degree of group solidarity achieved made for some resentment. Even though these things were true, the subgroups worked faithfully, and members of the total group began to become well acquainted with one another.

During the summer vacation following the organization of the three subgroups a new director of instruction was appointed in Denver. He became the local coordinator of the leadership project. Although he had not been involved previously, he had taken an active part in earlier Denver work with the Institute and had been watching the leadership study with interest. Largely on his own initiative he decided, for several reasons, that the three subgroups should be discontinued and a new approach tried. It now seems surprising that such a significant decision as this should have been made unilaterally and that the group should have accepted it without strong protest.

In the fall of 1949, when work on the leadership study was resumed, individual school projects were selected as a focus for further work. The principal and the coordinator of each school identified some pressing problem requiring improved instructional leadership in their own school and tried to solve this problem. Differing interests led a few principals and coordinators to choose projects on which they worked individually rather than cooperatively. One or two teams were prevented by the press of other duties from working on the project chosen.

A fuller description of the projects undertaken appears in the next chapter. It will be sufficient to state here that, in general, this kind of teamwork proved effective and was used throughout the remainder of the leadership study. Even more important, work on many of the building team projects is continuing even though the leadership study has been officially terminated.

The total group continued to meet until the end of the leadership study. The meetings were devoted primarily to formulating purposes, establishing "bench marks," measuring growth and change in insights and attitudes, listening to presentations of reports, observing prepared activities, engaging in occasional role-playing, and summarizing and drawing conclusions.

Subgroup activity, after the initiation of the building team projects, was for limited periods of time and in connection with specific topics or activities only. Membership in these interim groups, as they became known, was open to any member of the total group who wished to participate. One interim group met early in 1950 to consider effective methods of working with parents; another, to study the methods of action research. Reading about and discussing leadership, examining and interpreting data, and criticizing the manuscripts resulting from the leadership study were some of the activities in which later interim groups engaged.

One activity considered especially significant was a five-day workshop held immediately after the close of school at the end of the second year of the project (1950). All the participants whose personal plans permitted them to remain in Denver—nineteen—attended, and the week was devoted to summarizing what had been done and planning cooperatively for future activities.

The number of committees was kept to a minimum, but some committee activity was found to be necessary. A steering committee planned for efficient use of available consultant time and provided general direction and encouragement for the leadership project. In the fall of 1949 a committee was established to prepare a bulletin of project activities. At the same time another committee began to compile a list of leadership techniques that had been tried and found effective. A committee was also appointed to handle details of the 1950 summer workshop.

The activities of the leadership project are discussed in greater detail in Chapter 6. What we learned about increasing the productivity of small groups—an aspect of leadership of great concern to us—is reported in Chapter 7. Data from a number of instruments used to obtain more objective information about our achievements are interpreted in Chapter 8.

6

PROJECT ACTIVITIES

The Denver leadership project included many different activities. Some were more successful than others. In this chapter a number of important things we learned from each activity and a few of the difficulties we faced as we worked together are discussed, and the reasons for successes and failures are commented on.

The Total Group

Throughout the project efforts were made to involve the participants in activities *as a total group.* This was done primarily because Denver experiences with studies limited to one school or to a small group of participants had not been entirely successful and also because the problem being investigated was one common to all the schools. That our work as a total group had beneficial concomitant effects is indicated by the fact that, in an evaluation of the project, the statement "We have become better acquainted as persons" ranked second on a list of twenty-seven achievements (see Chapter 8, p. 178).

Formulating and Clarifying Purposes

One of the important functions of the total group was to formulate and clarify general purposes, which guided the activities of smaller groups. Perhaps the value of this function is more clearly seen in retrospect than it was at the time of the leadership study, when the total group's lack of information about specific building projects was sometimes criticized. The existence of the total group, however, and its relatively frequent meetings, prevented various smaller groups from losing sight of the primary purpose of the study. All the participants became better acquainted, problems were more clearly defined, and whatever misunderstandings had existed at first were gradually dissipated by cooperative effort.

Establishing "Bench Marks"

Another function of the total group was to establish "bench marks" for the study's achievements. All our efforts in this area were made in meetings of the total group. When we had an opportunity to discuss, as a group, the significance of what we had done, we wrote our periodic evaluations more thoughtfully and willingly.

The longer we worked together, the more important it seemed to us to know what our conceptions, understandings, and practices had been when we started. Toward the end of the project we attempted to secure this information, and at that time we were at a loss to understand why we had resisted getting it sooner. Several participants, who had had research experience, tried to help us see the importance of this kind of data throughout the project, but it took us a long time to recognize the need for it. Our research design did not become entirely clear until the study had been almost completed. Attempts to delineate research methodology were relatively ineffective until the group had floun-

112

dered enough to see the need for it. Helping a group become aware of the importance of a research design for the solution of practical problems is difficult, and we were only moderately successful in fostering this awareness.

There were several reasons for resistance to a systematic research design. Even though specific problems had not been clearly defined, we were anxious to improve our leadership, and the consideration of research methodology seemed a time-consuming, impractical diversion. In addition, the painstaking process of defining a problem, stating action hypotheses, taking the actions, obtaining data, and formulating generalizations seemed to require technical abilities we did not possess. Finally, we tended at first to concentrate on specific symptoms and techniques. Only after a great deal of work did we begin to realize that many specific difficulties were actually related manifestations of the same broad, general problems.

Listening and Reacting to Reports

Another activity of the total group was listening to and discussing reports. During the workshop held in the summer of 1950 one of the consultants presented a statement concerning the relation between perception and behavior and the implications of this relation for instructional leadership (see Chapter 3, p. 49–51). The group took a half day to discuss this statement, and the reaction of those present was that both it and the subsequent discussion were extremely helpful. As a result of this experience, plans were made to include reports and discussions in most subsequent meetings of the total group. Some of the reports were presented by subgroup spokesmen and described achievements and problems. Others were concerned with ideas about leadership or research methodology. Our ability to see the interrelatedness of the things we were doing seemed to increase with the initiation of these reports.

The total group was interested in the activities and findings of subgroups and committees. After the three original subgroups had been discontinued, all subgroups and committees were authorized by the total group and organized as part of that body. It was clearly implied that they were expected to report back to the total group. The reports helped to clarify subgroup tasks, keep the focus on the central problems of the leadership study, stimulate work on subgroup projects, and maintain a sense of involvement on the part of all the participants in the many activities being carried on. The element of competition was minimized, and members were encouraged to participate in activities in accordance with their interests and the time they had available.

Some problems, of course, arose in connection with the reports. Chief among these was our difficulty in communicating with one another. It is not easy to realize, after one has been through a learning experience, that describing the results to others is not enough. They must develop some feeling for the experience itself if a report of results is to have significance. For example, one subgroup had tried out many different ways of recording minutes of meetings in an attempt to develop a form that would summarize questions raised, discussions held, decisions reached, and assignments accepted as a result of decisions. The work had been carefully done, and the form eventually devised had been tried and found effective. In the report that was given, however, only the final form was presented and explained. Those giving the report were at a loss to understand the total group's indifference until a careful analysis revealed the fundamental weakness noted above. Subsequently, greater care was taken by subgroups to include in their reports some information about the learning experience as a whole.

Engaging in Role-Playing

Another technique that provides a group with a common experience and focuses the attention of all on the same problem is role-playing. Although we did not use this technique very often, the immediate reaction to every role-playing experience was very favorable. One of the situations we role-played, which centered around a status leader confronted with a group decision different from his own, is described in some detail here.

Problem: Leader reaction to a group decision different from his own.

Situation: At a regular meeting of the policy committee of Wilson High School (1,000 students) the principal explains that it is necessary to raise $200 to finance the trip of a member of the student council to an important student council meeting in Boston. (Fare, $156. Other expenses, $44.) He is convinced that presenting an all-school operetta is the best way of raising the money. Although the school operetta was discontinued last year because of the great strain it placed on the school program, the principal feels that it should be revived and used as a money-raising device.

In the past about 125 Wilson students have put on the operetta. The entertainment has always been well patronized by the community. It is sure income. However, most of the staff members on the policy committee oppose the operetta. Only one teacher supports the principal. One other teacher is indifferent to the whole matter.

The decision must be made at once if the production is to be ready before the school year ends and the money is needed.

Roles: THE PRINCIPAL—An engaging, attractive person, the principal has considerable influence as a leader in his school. He is eager to use the operetta to raise the necessary money. When he meets opposition to his plan, he exercises every bit of his talent to win the committee to his point of view. But he is perfectly capable of changing his mind, of seeking alternatives, of incorporating objections into his plans. He wants to effect a compromise, if possible, if he should be unable to have his own way entirely.

115

THE MUSIC TEACHER—A capable woman, the music teacher has enjoyed putting on operettas in the past; but she is so discouraged by the problems of production that she is against trying another one.

THE ENGLISH TEACHER—Convinced of the great importance of his subject in the lives of his students, this teacher is resolutely opposed to an operetta. Such productions always take students out of classes and interfere with homework.

THE MATHEMATICS TEACHER—The mathematics teacher agrees with the English teacher in his opposition to the operetta.

THE SCIENCE TEACHER—This teacher agrees with the principal, more to win favor with the administration than because he feels strongly about the importance of the principal's plans.

THE COMMERCIAL TEACHER—The commercial teacher is rather bored with the whole thing. She doesn't care one way or the other. Neither the principal nor the other members of the committee look to her for support or interest.

Time and Place: The meeting takes place in the social room of the school after a busy school day. It is early April.

In order to analyze the role-playing, those who had no assigned roles were divided into three groups and briefed as follows:

Group A: Pay particular attention to the techniques of the leader as he meets resistance. What does he do? What might he do?

Group B: Try to identify the roles that are played by the different people in the situation.

Group C: Pay particular attention to what seems to be the motivation of the role-players representing teachers. Why do they say what they say? What is the effect of their statements on the principal?

The actual role-playing lasted about fifteen minutes, and the discussion for an hour and a half. The post-meeting evaluations indicated that it had been a very successful session. The following are some of the learnings reported by members of the group:

> Don't put members of a group on the defensive. Actually *listen* to what others say. Let other people point out why an alternative plan will not work.
>
> As a member of the cast, and as one who played a role different from my own, I learned much about how an objector feels.
>
> It was good for me to have pointed out that the principal *did* have leads he didn't follow up. I miss them, too, and will be on the lookout for them in the future (I hope).
>
> People are motivated by different things. To try to understand the motivation is important.
>
> We seem to be willing to use democratic means when we are able to do so and still gain our own ends. If there is conflict, we are prone to junk the democratic means and hold on to our original ideas.

After this role-playing experience members of the group reported that they had actually practiced in real situations some of the things they had learned. The modification in behavior came with difficulty, but the effort was worth while. We began to indicate, by our actions, our growing realization that differences in point of view might be due to more than mere obstinacy.

Drawing Conclusions

Meetings of the total group provided a valuable opportunity for examining what had been done and drawing whatever conclusions seemed warranted. One effective method of consolidating learnings was to have a member of the group, usually a consultant from the Horace Mann-Lincoln Institute or the director of instruction, present in written form what seemed to be the major generalizations growing out of certain aspects of our work. The group then

117

read this statement and discussed its validity critically. The first four chapters of this book are, in large part, the result of this kind of critical analysis.

The Subgroups

There were great variations in background, training, experience, interest, ability, and point of view among the participants in the Denver study. In addition, the kind of study undertaken, although directed toward one general goal, involved intensive, detailed work and many different responsibilities. For both reasons it was decided to divide the total group into several subgroups. As has been said, subgroups were established by the total group and were responsible to it.

Original Subgroups

The first three subgroups that were established investigated problems related to (1) leadership in in-service education, (2) group process, and (3) specific leadership procedures. Because of differences in the problems under investigation and variations in working methods, one subgroup considered its work done while another was just getting started. Dissatisfactions began to be felt. Although all reported to the total group, a feeling of rivalry rather than cooperation resulted. No definite plans had been made for relating the work of the subgroups to the task of the total group. As a result of these and other difficulties, the subgroups were abandoned during the summer of 1949.

Interim Groups

After the original subgroups had been abandoned, a new method of dividing into smaller groups had to be found. It was felt that if subgroups were to be successful, (1) each subgroup formed should be open to any member of the total

118

group who wished to participate; (2) any participant in the study should feel free to work with all subgroups in whose work he was interested; (3) membership in subgroups should be entirely voluntary; (4) all subgroups should be authorized by the total group and should report back to that body.

As has already been mentioned, the result was the formation of interim groups. The first of these included everyone working with parent organizations. The Denver schools were being attacked, at the time, for their supposed lack of attention to the teaching of "fundamentals"; and school officials were concerned about the misunderstanding or indifference shown by many of the patrons of the schools. Apparently the usual methods of explaining and winning support for the school program had not resulted in the understanding that had been hoped for. Consequently, working with parents to arrive at mutual understanding regarding educational purposes was viewed as an important aspect of instructional leadership. The members of this interim group, who had tried various methods of working with parent organizations, met to exchange experiences, criticize procedures, interpret data, and draw whatever conclusions seemed warranted. Many of the generalizations appearing in the next chapter are a result of these meetings. Interest was high. Conclusions seemed tangible and helpful.

At about this time many of us began to develop greater interest in action research as a method of improving instructional leadership. Arrangements were made for the formation of an interim group to study action research procedures. Meeting three times, the group considered the formulation of hypotheses, the development of instruments for securing data, the analysis of data, and the nature of generalizations. Since they had had training in research techniques and previous experience with action research, the Institute consultants and the director of instruction served as resource persons for this interim group. Because it was focused on the current activities of the leadership project, the consideration of techniques and procedures had a concreteness and clarity that abstract discussions had lacked. The result of this group's activity was an increased interest in research methodology on the part of all the participants in the project, and this in turn led to an improvement in the design of many project activities.

After a great deal of discussion and work, much of it distressingly slow in producing results, we realized that changing behavior was more difficult than we had supposed. In order to understand what was involved when we tried to change our behavior, we decided to try to obtain some information that would help us answer the question, How much have we changed as a result of our study of instructional leadership? An interim group was formed to identify and list the improved practices that had been put into effect.

The same interim group on leadership practices spent considerable time studying two issues of the *Journal of Social Issues* in preparation for a seminar discussion. One of the issues was entitled "The Dynamics of the Discussion Group";[1] the other, "Consultant Role and Organizational Leadership: Improving Human Relations in Industry."[2] The discussion eventually focused on an article by Irving R. Knickerbocker[3] and was very successful. It contributed appreciably to our conceptualization of leadership as presented in Part I of this book.

In the course of the project we developed and adapted a number of instruments in order to obtain some quantitative data concerning our work and its effects. Analysis of the data obtained became the responsibility of interim groups. Announcements were sent to all participants in the

[1] *Journal of Social Issues*, 4:1–75, Spring 1948.
[2] *Ibid.*, 1–53, Summer 1948.
[3] Irving R. Knickerbocker, "Leadership: A Conception and Some Implications," *Journal of Social Issues*, 4:23–40, Summer 1948.

study when data summaries were ready. All who were interested then met to analyze the data and formulate generalizations from them. Membership varied from one time to another, but a substantial number of participants was present at each meeting. A clearer understanding of both the nature of the project and its accomplishments resulted from the work of these groups.

We devoted a full school year to bringing the leadership project to a formal close and preparing a report. All of us accepted some degree of responsibility for the final manuscript. As sections were drafted, interim groups met to criticize them and make suggestions for improvement. These activities gave us a clearer picture of what we had accomplished, what we had failed to do, and what we might do differently if we were to undertake the same kind of project again.

It seemed to us that the interim groups fulfilled their function adequately. They enabled us to work, according to the time at our disposal, on those aspects of the general problem of greatest interest to us. If this study were to be repeated, we would make use of this form of organization again.

Committees

As might be expected in any group as large as ours, certain responsibilities could be discharged only if specific assignment of duties was made. Although the interim groups met part of this need, some committee assignments were also found necessary. The general planning for each of the visits of the consultants and the organizational responsibility for the project as a whole were assigned to a steering committee. This committee was composed of representatives of each of the groups participating in the project—junior high school coordinators, senior high school coordinators, junior high school principals, senior high school principals, and central office personnel. The committee planned the tentative agenda for each visit of the consultants, developed post-meeting evaluation questionnaires for meetings of the total group, and prepared summaries of the reactions obtained. In addition, it took care of the details connected with such tasks as the establishment of interim groups.

Early in the study we recognized the need for systematically recording our learnings. A leadership techniques committee was appointed to pull together, organize, and summarize the experience of all the participants with various leadership techniques. After a year of study and revision the committee presented a list of seventy-four techniques and concepts that had been tested and found valuable by one or more participants. The techniques and concepts were organized under the following headings: (1) Planning and Preparing for Group Meetings, (2) Selecting Group Members, (3) Presiding at Group Meetings, (4) Facilitating Communication, (5) Aiding Group Decisions and Action, (6) Encouraging Participation, (7) Sharing Leadership with Group Members, (8) Evaluating Group Meetings, (9) Improving Group Processes, (10) Improving Human Relations. The eventual result of the activity of the committee was a questionnaire that provided the basis for much of our final evaluation of the project (see Chapter 8, p. 179–193).

Certain specific tasks also called for short-term committee assignments. For example, one committee made all arrangements for the summer workshop of 1950, and these arrangements did much to promote the success of the workshop.

Working in groups—whether in interim groups, committees, or the total group—provided many opportunities for testing the hypotheses we had formulated regarding leadership. We tried to discover why some meetings went well and others did not. Certain procedures used by the chairman or other members seemed to facilitate the work of the group;

others seemed to hinder it. We tried to identify these different procedures and to analyze them. As has been said, however, we became restive whenever a consideration of group process seemed to interfere with the job at hand; and we learned more and more to think of process as a means, not an end.

The Workshop

Nineteen participants found it possible to meet during the week following the close of school in June, 1950, for concentrated work on specific problems. The workshop proved successful for a number of reasons. First, there were no interruptions or outside pressures. All the other activities connected with the leadership study were carried on while we were fulfilling our regular school responsibilities. Second, we found in the workshop companionship and support. Although each of us presumably could have devoted a similar period of time to project activities if the workshop had not been organized, we probably would not have done so. In any event, we would have missed the stimulation that comes from working with a group on common problems. Third, since both Institute consultants participated in the workshop, we had a chance to raise questions and work out cooperatively what seemed to us to be good answers. All of us learned to understand one another better and developed a better working relationship. Finally, in contrast with the periodic meetings of the total group, which were necessarily limited in scope, the workshop gave us a chance to engage in a variety of activities and to discover how the things we did were related to one another. As a result, we were able to see much more clearly the interrelatedness of many other project activities and to appreciate their contribution to our central task.

The Building Teams

Early in the Denver study we recognized that effective instructional leadership was most likely to be developed through practice in the school situation. Plans were therefore made to inaugurate in each of the secondary schools a project on which the school's principal and instructional coordinator would work as a team. It was felt that in this way realistic situations would be provided for testing promising hypotheses.

The amount of progress made on these projects varied considerably from school to school. Differences in the urgency of the problem identified, in the interest the team had in it, in the staff's reaction to initial steps, and in the time available for work helped to explain this variation. The most important reason, however, seemed to be related to personnel. New principals were assigned to all five senior high schools as well as several junior high schools during the three years of the study. These changes inevitably interfered with completion of some of the building projects.

Kinds of Problems Studied

Perhaps the best way of indicating the kinds of problems studied by the building teams is to list the action hypotheses they proposed to test.

1. Staff participation in interpreting data from a student questionnaire will increase teachers' understanding of school objectives.

2. Cooperatively working out, one at a time, the problems faced in teaching integrated courses will help teachers master the fundamentals of unit teaching.

3. A study by the teaching staff of reasons for students' dropping out of school will lead to improvements in the high school curriculum.

124

4. Helping teachers to identify and work on their problems will result in improved morale.

5. Involving parents, administrators, teachers, and students in the planning of a controversial unit of study—sex education—will result in its successful introduction.

6. Making professional literature readily available to teachers will help them with their teaching problems.

7. Identification of guidance problems by teachers and their cooperative work toward the solution of these problems will tend to integrate guidance with the total school program.

8. Identification by teachers of instructional areas requiring modification and their determination of methods of bringing about needed changes will lead to curriculum improvement.

9. Training sessions will increase the competence of leaders, recorders, and resource persons in PTA groups.

10. If the status leader limits his comments in staff committee meetings to (a) clarifying the statements of others, (b) reflecting the feelings of members, (c) raising questions, (d) pointing out resources, and (e) calling attention to some elements of group process that may facilitate the work of the group, he will help group members assume greater responsibility for meetings.

11. The amount of participation in parent-teacher meetings will be increased and the quality of discussion improved by (a) asking parents at the end of each meeting to indicate topics they would like to have discussed at the next meeting, (b) dividing the total group into smaller discussion groups to consider questions of particular interest to them, and (c) getting parents' suggestions for the improvement of meetings.

12. Ascertaining how teachers feel about grade planning meetings will provide a basis for improving these meetings.

13. Consistent practice and evaluation of certain group

work procedures will result in more effective grade planning meetings.

14. School-wide emphasis on certain fundamentals will result in improved student performance in these fundamentals.

15. Assumption by the coordinator of responsibility for physical arrangements in connection with staff meetings —room scheduling, seating accommodations, materials, mimeographing—will result in more productive meetings.

Each of these hypotheses pertained to an important problem in the school, and each seemed capable of solution under local conditions.

Techniques and Procedures

Defining problems. Although the specific procedures used in the building projects were almost as varied as the projects themselves, many of the generalizations that grew out of our work as a total group were applied. The usual way of beginning work on a project was to define the problem as concretely as possible. Many coordinators and principals used check lists and questionnaires for this purpose. One school, which was working with parent groups that had been somewhat critical of the general education program, approached the definition of the problem somewhat indirectly. Parents were asked to indicate the degree of importance they attached to each of a series of activities and learnings. Some were considered more important than others by the parents. The problem was then defined as *How can the school foster these important activities and learnings?* rather than *What is good or bad about the general education program?*

In another school, where an investigation was being made of the contribution reading of professional literature could make to the solution of instructional problems, the definition of the problem was approached more directly. The following request was sent to staff members:

126

Several teachers have indicated that they would like to read more professional literature if it were not so difficult to obtain. I have undertaken the project of securing material from various sources and channeling it to these teachers. If you would like to have material channeled to you, indicate on the blank below the kind of material you are interested in, and I will see what I can find. Most of the material will be in the form of brief magazine articles.

The responses to this request defined the problem for the coordinator in terms of both the extent and the nature of staff interest.

One team, which was working on the improvement of the curriculum, attempted to approach problem definition through an analysis of job functions. A rather long and complicated instrument was used for this purpose.

Some of the attempts to define problems were more informal. One coordinator, who was trying to increase the satisfaction teachers in her school derived from their work, defined the problem in terms of what had proved satisfying to her—receiving credit for work done, having an opportunity to exercise initiative, being dealt with fairly, and so on. These were the things she concentrated on in her attempt to solve the problem.

Another approach to problem definition was analysis of data. This method was used in one school, where a summary of former students' replies to a questionnaire concerning their feelings and ideas about the school was given to the teaching staff. The teachers then used this material as a basis for defining instructional problems that needed investigation.

Formulating hypotheses. The hypotheses listed on pages 124–126 were not developed quickly. Each was formulated after considerable thought. Our procedure was to examine the defined problems carefully for clues to possible solutions. Using the term *hunch* almost synonymously with *hypothesis*

127

helped us to get started on this phase of the research process. We learned, however, that a hunch, to be useful to us as a hypothesis, had to fulfill two conditions. First, the action implied had to be feasible—capable of being put into practice. For example, the hypothesis *If more teachers were allocated to this school, participation in curriculum work would increase* seemed reasonable, but the action implied was one we could not easily take. Larger staffs cost money. The tax rate in Denver was already high, and the impending influx of children into the schools meant that the maintenance of existing teacher-student ratios would seriously strain the school district's resources. The hunch about adding teachers to a staff might be a good one in theory, but it was one we could not put into practice. On the other hand, the action implied by the hypothesis *If I refrain from introducing new ideas in group meetings, participation by the other members will increase* was one we could take. The factors in this situation were within our control, and we were able to experiment with them.

Second, the hypothesis had to be testable. For example, the possibility of testing the hypothesis *Analysis of case studies will increase teachers' sensitivity to the needs of adolescents* depended on our ability to measure sensitivity to adolescent needs. Because no adequate instruments for this kind of measurement were available, the hypothesis could not be tested even though the situation was within our control.

We concluded that to be testable, a hypothesis must meet two conditions:

1. *The predicted consequences of a presumably desirable action must be capable of manifestation in some form of modified behavior.* We realized that changes might be manifested in many ways and that new attitudes, feelings, and knowledge all lead to behavior modification.

128

2. The predicted consequences must be capable of being observed or measured. We do not wish here to contrast "subjective" methods of observation with "objective" methods, since both serve useful purposes in social investigations. However, the observations on which conclusions are based must be observations of behavior directly related to the conditions of the hypothesis.

Collecting data. The problem, once a hypothesis has been stated and plans have been made for taking the actions implied, becomes one of obtaining evidence concerning results. We gave a great deal of attention to the characteristics of adequate data. We recognized the importance of securing data directly related to the hypothesis being tested. Whenever possible, we tried to obtain data in a form that would make possible comparison with other data. We realized that one testing of a hypothesis is usually not enough—repeated testing is necessary. We became aware of the importance of timing in the collection of data. We recognized that, if they are informed, opinions can be used as evidence. Finally, we realized that the collection of data is not an end in itself and should stop when the necessary evidence has been secured.

Some of our sources of data (in addition, of course, to the questionnaire) were the following:

Free discussion, with particular attention to *why* or *because* statements

Cooperative records (particularly useful in establishing "bench marks")

Tape recordings (particularly useful in determining and comparing emotional tone, but somewhat voluminous and possibly frustrating)

Profile charts

Statements of opinion (particularly useful in comparing feelings)

129

Anecdotal records
Post-meeting reactions
Minutes of meetings
Interviews
Interaction charts

Interpreting data. The ease with which we were able to interpret data was proportional to the care with which they had been secured. If the hypotheses were testable, if the requirements for testing them had been clearly recognized, and if information had been secured with these requirements in mind, interpreting data proved less difficult. If, on the other hand—and this sometimes happened—the requirements for testing the hypotheses had not been clearly recognized and information had been obtained only because it was readily available, interpretation became a much more difficult, if not impossible, task.

Because ours were studies of social action, we could not hope to control or even recognize all the variables that might be involved in any one situation. Social situations are dynamic, not static. Every problem is a function of the situation in which it arises, and the fact that a group is working on a problem changes the nature of the problem itself. New elements are brought into the situation, and these have to be considered in drawing conclusions. In one school, for example, the principal and coordinator decided to test the following hypothesis: *If teachers identify instructional areas requiring modification and determine methods of bringing about needed changes, the curriculum will improve.* Accordingly, each step in the selection of areas needing modification and in the definition of problems was taken by the entire staff. Opportunities for individual as well as group work within the areas selected were provided. Every teacher seemed to find a place for himself in the process. Many badly needed changes in the curriculum were brought about.

130

In the light of the data collected, we concluded that the hypothesis had been supported. The coordinator, however, pointed out that another factor might have been involved. She said, "I am not sure whether there will be any lasting effects. I sometimes wonder whether it isn't the interest of the leaders that holds such a project together." The recognition of this element in effect suggested a new hypothesis to be tested.

Techniques and procedures are constantly being developed for dealing with the multiple variables in an experimental situation. We in Denver had not the time, nor did we feel the need, to study and perfect these techniques. We tried to keep our hypotheses simple and clear-cut and, through cooperative formulation of generalizations, attempted to take into consideration as many of the elements of a situation as possible in drawing conclusions.

Generalizing. Each of the building projects was undertaken to meet a specific need, and for two reasons we have not attempted to summarize here the findings pertaining to each of the hypotheses listed on pages 124–126. First, the projects are in different stages of completion. Some have been concluded, and reports of them have already been published. Some were halted midway because of personnel changes in the schools or other difficulties.

Second, although the projects were vital to us, we feel that the inclusion of specific findings would not contribute materially to the reader's understanding of instructional leadership. Most of the generalizations concerning the nature and improvement of leadership have already been presented in Part I of this book; and we would like to draw attention here to only a few relatively concrete and yet widely applicable learnings.

One of the important generalizations that grew out of several of the building projects was that it is essential to define problems specifically. For example, in one of the schools the best way of improving the conduct of students had been debated for years. It seemed almost impossible to reach agreement about what to do or even about what constituted desirable conduct. The problem was again tackled during the Denver study. The staff worked out scales for rating student behavior, and these were used in classroom, laboratory, hall, and lunchroom situations. The staff also developed some scales to measure attitudes, scholarship, and school loyalty. As a result of the use of these scales, judgments based on personal, subjective criteria tended to disappear, and problems were much more specifically identified. The ratings enabled teachers to offer definite help to students, and this resulted in marked improvement in conduct.

Another generalization supported by evidence from the various projects was that moving ahead one step at a time is preferable to attempting to do too much at once. In one school the principal and coordinator were meeting great resistance from some of the teachers required to teach integrated courses. Expounding on the advantages of unit teaching helped little. The procedure in this case involved working out one at a time problems faced in teaching integrated courses. The teachers worked out these problems cooperatively and reported afterward that they had derived a great deal of satisfaction as well as help from the project.

A third generalization growing out of the building projects was that studies of other aspects of school life frequently motivate efforts to improve instruction. Such activities as the conduct study already mentioned, an investigation of the reasons for students' dropping out of school, the organization of a new school, studies to improve staff meetings— all led to more thorough examination of the instructional program.

A final generalization we would like to mention grew out of our work with parent-teacher groups. In the course of this work we realized that democratic procedures cannot be used to mask undemocratic motives. Going through the motions of cooperatively determining goals and means when the status leader had already decided on the course of action to be followed invariably led to difficulties. The spirit as well as the form of democracy is necessary if the values inherent in mutual goals-means leadership are to be realized.

Contributions of the Consultants

The two consultants participated in the building projects from their inception. Each agreed to work with half of the schools. During visits of the consultants, time was scheduled for individual conferences with the various building teams. These conferences were usually about one hour long, but flexibility in time was provided for. Between the consultants' visits to Denver they carried on extensive correspondence with the building teams.

The consultants made at least four important contributions to the projects. First, they provided stimulation and encouragement. The fact that commitments had been made to the consultant spurred the school teams on to action that sometimes they might not otherwise have taken. The consultants, in turn, encouraged the building teams in their work, especially when things were not going well.

Second, each school was able to use the consultant associated with its project as a resource person. Because part of their time was definitely allocated to the leadership study, because they could make available some of the other resources of Teachers College, and because they were familiar with educational theory and practice and had participated in similar experiments before, the consultants were able to render valuable assistance.

Third, the consultants, familiar with the Denver school situation but not part of it, were able to examine project activities much more objectively than we were. This objectivity helped us to keep our perspective and gave us greater confidence in our findings than we would otherwise have had.

Finally, the consultants helped us recognize the inter-relatedness of our various activities. It would have been easy for each building team to feel unique and alone, but because each of the consultants was associated with half of the projects and both were familiar with all projects, they were able to point out similarities without making evaluative comparisons. The knowledge that others were having similar experiences gave us support and enabled us to share our ideas and experiences more freely with one another.

Difficulties Encountered

Although we benefited greatly from our work on the building projects, difficulties did arise. Few of us found the time in our already crowded schedules to do as much as we would have liked to do. Time requirements should have been more carefully appraised before we embarked on the projects.

Another difficulty resulted from the fact that there were wide differences in the degree of enthusiasm we felt for the kind of research we were trying to do. We tried to anticipate this variation and plan activities so that no one would feel compelled to participate. Nevertheless, statements indicating a feeling of guilt for lack of interest were made from time to time. To the extent that our planning led to this feeling, it was poor planning.

A third difficulty we faced was the rather extensive shifting of personnel during the study. None of the persons newly assigned to a school was able to continue work on the building project that had been selected and begun before his assignment. This was completely understandable, but the projects suffered as a result.

A final serious difficulty not seen in our planning was that the decision to concentrate on building projects tended to exclude central office participants from one of the major activities of the study. It was expected that they would work on one or more of the projects or form a team of their own. Neither of these expectations was fulfilled. The one attempt that was made to organize central office participants in a cooperative study of a common problem was unsuccessful.

In spite of these and other difficulties and shortcomings, however, we feel that our work on the building projects resulted in improved behavior on our part and improved conditions in our schools; and we believe that it gave us a much clearer understanding of leadership functions in school situations.

The Consultants

It took a certain amount of time and effort for all of us to learn to work together. The Denver participants—principals, coordinators, and central office personnel—were anxious to learn about leadership. However, they were uncertain about what constituted leadership, how it was manifested, and how it could be appraised. They felt that the consultants, with their wider experience and training, would transmit to them the understandings and skills they lacked.

The consultants felt strongly that social problems are a function of the situation in which they arise. They believed that insight and understanding come as a result of participation and practice, not verbalization alone. They were convinced that learnings could have significance for the participants in the study only if they grew out of the actual school situation in Denver.

As a result of these divergent points of view, the early Denver meetings were only moderately successful. The consultants felt that a probing of the Denver situation through a problem census was essential to effective work. The Denver

135

people felt that they had talked about their problems for years. They wanted to know how these problems were related to leadership and how they could improve their leadership. They found it difficult to accept consultants who were not more aggressive. The consultants, on the other hand, found it difficult to realize that all members of the group did not share their enthusiasm for research. They misunderstood what the Denver people meant when they had agreed to participate in the leadership project.

The Denver group and the consultants really began to understand one another during the workshop held in the summer of 1950. At that time a talk given by one of the consultants concerning the relation between perception and behavior and the implications of this relation for instructional leadership was enthusiastically received. From then on the consultants assumed a more active role in the project, and the Denver people began to assume greater responsibility for their participation in it.

It is apparent now that if the consultants had helped to clarify, early in the project, the nature of leadership, the characteristics of action research, and the importance of studying instructional leadership in the Denver situation itself, the study would have had a more auspicious beginning. If, in addition, the Denver people had had a clearer understanding of what participation in the project would involve in respect to activity and time, and if they had been more willing to proceed on their own, the study would have been a more successful one.

The consultants and the Denver participants learned much from one another about working together. The cordial relations that exist after three years of intensive cooperative work is one of the important by-products of the study.

7

LEADERSHIP IN
SMALL FACE-TO-FACE GROUPS

A great deal of the work undertaken to improve the school curriculum is done by committees or other small face-to-face groups. These groups may consist of a variety of personnel, depending on the task to be accomplished. In the Denver project we worked with groups composed of teachers, status leaders, teachers and status leaders, teachers and parents, and teachers and students.

It has been increasingly recognized that curriculum revision by small groups whose members are directly affected by the problems under consideration results in greater general improvement than curriculum revision by a few status leaders. Our emphasis on cooperative group work resulted from our belief that those who must carry out decisions should participate in making the decisions and that active involvement is essential to both individual and group development.

As we experimented with ways of increasing the productivity of small working groups, we became convinced that the role played by the status leader—the principal, coordinator, superintendent, or supervisor—was especially important. Ordinarily, he is the one who can set the tone of the meeting, take the initiative in establishing a good working atmosphere, and assume initial responsibility for helping group members improve their methods of work. His skill in working with a group is a crucial factor, not only in his success as a leader, but also in the success of the group in achieving what it sets out to do. As we have said in earlier chapters, the extent to which he is able to help the group clarify its goals and develop methods of achieving them determines the effectiveness of his leadership. Familiarity with efficient group work procedures and problem solving methods and the ability to foster free expression and effective communication are essential if he is to provide this kind of assistance.

Our conception of the status leader's role implies that he must work with the group as a participant, not as a director of group activities. We were convinced that when a status leader works with a group in this way, there is the greatest possibility of developing the creativeness, resourcefulness, and initiative of group members as well as an atmosphere that encourages experimentation with promising new ideas. Although we did not find this conception of leadership very difficult to develop, we had great difficulty in learning to practice the behavior it implies. We found that the status leader who works with a group as a participant rather than a director may face serious difficulties unless the other members of the group share his views about leadership. Because the conception of instructional leadership elaborated here is a relatively new one, the status leader's interest in helping the group make its own decisions and carry out and appraise the actions these imply may be interpreted as a refusal to accept responsibilities that have always been associated with status leadership.

This chapter is a report of some of the things we learned

138

about increasing the productivity of small face-to-face groups. In summarizing our learnings, we have tried to emphasize implications that seem to be of general interest to curriculum workers.

Committee Formation

We have already referred briefly to the relation between the task a group has before it and the membership of the group. Presumably the people who take part in the activities of a particular working group should be those who are concerned about a common problem. The groups with which we worked were trying to accomplish a variety of tasks— select textbooks, plan the scope and sequence of curriculum units, budget the money allocated for purchase of instructional materials, interpret the implications of test results for curriculum improvement, set up procedures for collecting fines. One of the problems to which we directed our attention early in the Denver project was how to determine the membership of a small group working on instructional problems.

A number of methods are used in public schools to form the various committees essential to the school's operation. The most common is to establish at the beginning of the school year a number of standing committees whose members are designated by the principal or some other status leader. This method of forming committees has become traditional; it takes little time, and it seems to be efficient. Many status leaders believe that the only way of distributing committee assignments fairly among staff members is appointment. The assumption is often made that some of the jobs that have to be done will not attract volunteers.

Those of us who were trying to improve the efficiency of small groups developed, for various reasons, a strong antipathy for this method of forming committees and a desire to discover better methods. We questioned, too, the significance of the tasks assigned many of the traditional standing committees. We noted that many of them had little to do. Sometimes much could have been done by persons interested in the committee's task, but these were not members of the group.

Our observation of this situation and our experience with interim groups in the leadership project convinced us of the value of volunteer committees—committees consisting of persons sincerely interested in the tasks their group was to accomplish.

Volunteer Committees

Teachers will volunteer to serve on a committee when its work seems significant to them. In one school the members of the social committee had for many years been named by the principal. He felt that assigning people to it was one way of getting work out of teachers who avoided all other extra duties. As a result, social activities in the school were perfunctory and dull. Because some of the teachers believed that those who volunteered to serve on a committee would take greater interest in its assigned task, arrangements were made to obtain signatures of volunteers for all the standing committees of the school. One teacher, signing her name at the top of the social committee list, said, "I've always wanted a chance to be on that committee." Teachers who liked to work with her—men as well as women—added their names. Soon a social committee of seven was making plans for a coffee room, a staff picnic, a Halloween square dance, and a Christmas school party for staff members and their families. The good fellowship built by a social committee whose members volunteered because they had *ideas* about social activities helped to weld the staff into a group that has been able to add several time-consuming curriculum revision projects to daily teaching schedules. In working

140

groups, members of the staff found that they were able to communicate more readily with one another because they knew one another socially as well as professionally.

We found that the principle of volunteering worked especially well when staff members understood the nature of important jobs. Frequently a status leader merely names the job he believes should be done and then is disappointed when no one seems interested in doing it. This practice on the part of status leaders, we concluded, is not a fair test of the principle of volunteering. In one of our schools the staff, engaged in the task of improving instruction, had, after a great deal of discussion, given priority to three problems. The entire staff understood the specific problems needing attention because these had been identified by small discussion groups involving all the teachers. It was recognized that three committees would be needed to study the problems considered most urgent and to recommend action. Persons interested in serving on any one of the three committees were asked to write their name and committee preference on a slip of paper and to put the slip into the coordinator's mailbox. Teachers did not know who else would be serving on the committee of their choice; it was the task that was of paramount importance. Fifteen from a staff of thirty-seven volunteered. Three indicated willingness to serve on either of two of the committees. The resulting reports were excellent because all fifteen volunteers were interested in what they were doing and consequently worked hard.

Appointed and Elected Committees

Individual interests. In many situations it was not possible to adopt completely the principle of volunteering. We found that committees could be appointed or elected in various ways and that they worked most efficiently when the interests and abilities of appointees or nominees were carefully determined and considered before appointments were

141

made. One of the schools experimented for two years with ways of making committee membership serve the needs of committee members as well as the best interests of the school. In this school a welfare committee composed of six members—elected representatives of the administrative, teaching, and custodial groups—concerned itself with all problems related to staff interests. For example, the committee considered such questions as the installation of a pay telephone; a more equitable distribution of extra jobs, special assignments, and clerical duties; the scheduling of a school rest period; the building of a school parking lot.

The welfare committee eventually came to serve as a nominating group for all school committees. Only those who had indicated willingness to serve were presented as nominees. Welfare committee members talked with each individual before a slate was drawn up and presented to the staff. Equitable distribution of responsibilities and "honors" was planned by the committee, and the staff elected its representatives from willing candidates.

Under this arrangement committee assignments were widely distributed. It had been customary for one person to serve on two or three important committees because others were thought to lack sufficient ability, interest, or willingness to take on added responsibilities. The new method of determining committee membership reduced ill will and tended to increase the sense of worth of those staff members who had felt before that their talents were not needed. All members of the staff were asked to serve in one capacity or another on committees that had important functions to fulfill. Although previously some positions had remained vacant through default, all committees have had full and active membership since this plan has been in operation.

Appropriate abilities. Thoughtful attention to the selection of committee members results in more efficient use of the abilities and skills of staff members. We found that committees were frequently appointed without serious consideration of (1) the kinds of abilities needed for a particular job or (2) the special abilities possessed by individual staff members.

In one school a difficult task—the rating of probationary teachers—was carried out satisfactorily when the principal requested help from the people whose interests and understandings made them most competent to give help. The ratings were mandatory, but the principal had never been satisfied with the criteria used or the materials employed to determine whether or not the criteria had been met. He therefore asked the probationary teachers to serve on a committee that would establish rating criteria and schedule the principal's evaluation visits and individual conferences. The list of criteria these teachers developed; the quantity of lesson plans, units, tests, and project materials they submitted; their feelings when the dates for visits and conferences approached; the anonymous descriptions they gave of their reactions to conferences—all attested to the success of the experiment.

Factors Influencing Method of Forming Committees

Our study convinced us that the most productive committees consist of members who volunteer to do a job they understand and are interested in. We realized, however, that circumstances sometimes preclude the exclusive use of volunteering as a method of forming small working groups.

Time. Often the time at which a committee must meet determines in part the people who can serve on it. For example, the Denver schools are committed to the principle of school work on school time, and most committees meet during periods that have been set aside during the school day to enable teachers to work in small groups on instructional problems. Six teachers free for such work during the third hour might wish to serve on six different committees.

143

Their choice is limited, however, because all those free at the same time must, of necessity, be members of the same committee or committees.

Special abilities. Frequently a person is asked to take special committee responsibilities because a status leader or staff member recognizes that he has the special abilities needed for a particular task. When the East District Articulation Committee, consisting of twenty-nine representatives of the elementary schools and the junior and senior high schools, met to elect its chairman for the year (a job no one seemed to want), it was recognized that one member of the group—an instructional coordinator—had, as a result of her participation in the leadership project, gained considerable insight into the importance of good interpersonal relations for committee work. She was nominated, and although the work was an additional load, the "compliment" pleased her and persuaded her to accept the responsibility. We found that when an individual's special abilities are discussed with him and he realizes that these are needed for carrying out a particular task, he is usually willing to accept the additional responsibility. The abilities of persons who are reluctant to volunteer can sometimes be made available in this way, and their potential leadership developed.

Social compatibility. A committee whose members have deliberately chosen to work together often does excellent work. Good interpersonal relations are usually conducive to getting a job done, and they facilitate communication among committee members. One eighth-grade teacher's suggestion that a study of all available standardized American history tests should be made in order to improve the evaluation of students was accepted by an eighth-grade planning group. The chairman of the group asked the teacher who had made the proposal to serve on a study committee and to select another member of the planning group as an associate. The teacher's interest in the problem and her choice of a con-

144

genial and able co-worker were important factors in the success of the study.

Task Identification

Anyone within a school—including, of course, the status leader—can and should call attention to the need for a small group to work on some instructional problem. We learned, however, that the best work is done when great freedom is permitted the group, once it has been constituted, to define its specific task within a broad area. Successful task identification requires that a substantial part of each meeting, and a proportionately greater part of early meetings, be devoted to agenda building. It requires also a permissive, free atmosphere, because only when such an atmosphere exists can the ideas of all members of the group be obtained and goals of significance and interest to everyone defined.

Task identification was an essential step in the work of all our small groups, and dissatisfaction with meetings usually resulted when goals had not been clearly defined by the members themselves. Unless agreement had been reached regarding purposes, no commonly accepted criteria existed by which the group could measure its achievement. We therefore tried to avoid having agenda set by steering committees, except in large groups. For subgroups to work on particular problems and report back to the total group was common, but we came more and more to feel that the specific tasks undertaken by such groups should be those of significance to the members themselves.

Cooperative Agenda Building

Successful group work requires time to (1) enumerate the specific tasks to be accomplished; (2) establish priorities among these tasks; and (3) look realistically at the limits within which the work must be done. When we began to

145

experiment in teacher planning groups with cooperative agenda building, our first efforts were directed toward helping members develop a willingness to make suggestions. Frequently we neglected to choose wisely among suggestions and to appraise each in terms of its time requirements.

Because most of us had taken so much initiative in meetings in the past, we were expected to continue to direct the activities of everyone. Although our conception of our role changed and we came to realize the value of shared responsibility, many of our co-workers continued to conform to the old pattern. As a result, we placed such great value on *some* participation in agenda building that we frequently began to discuss items in the order in which they had been suggested without taking time to establish criteria for choosing among them. Sometimes we did not have time to discuss all the items proposed. Consequently, we were considered by our working associates to be intentionally overlooking some agenda proposals, encouraging without any particular reason the discussion of items in the order in which they had been suggested, and refusing to accept sufficient responsibility for the success or failure of meetings. Eventually we learned to submit all proposed items to group members for their reactions and to plan the working agenda on the basis of their choices. This was one way of assuring more careful consideration of all suggestions, and it meant that the status leader shared responsibility for planning and achievement with other members of the group.

To prevent anyone from feeling that his suggestion had been ignored, we experimented with ways of adopting agenda through group action. The recorder or other designated person would list on the board all items suggested for consideration. The chairman would then propose more than one way of proceeding, if possible, and ask for other suggestions. The group then adopted or rejected the various items and established priorities among them. Everyone's

146

ideas about the agenda were considered; and items were included, postponed, or eliminated by group decision. The leader assumed no more responsibility for decisions than any other group member.

We found that before items of business are selected, the following questions must be considered realistically by the group: (1) How much can we do in a forty-five minute planning session? (2) Shall we limit the agenda or find ways of extending the time? (3) What tentative time allotment do we propose for each item to be considered?

As we have said, the importance of these questions in connection with agenda building was not seen at first. Consequently, we often implied by our list of "things to do" that we had a great deal more than forty-five minutes at our disposal. We were then forced to overlook a number of items or hurry through the last few, and both courses left us somewhat frustrated. With practice, however, we learned to predict more accurately how much time each job would require, and our satisfaction with meetings increased correspondingly.

Methods of building agenda cooperatively. The more we experimented, the clearer it became that the agenda-building aspect of group work is also influenced by situational factors. Because getting the ideas of all group members into the open is so important, we tried to avoid routinizing the procedure for obtaining items of business. Several of the methods we found effective are listed below.

1. In advance of a called meeting the chairman circulates a sheet of paper on which he has listed one or two items of recognized importance in order to stimulate the thinking of other group members, who are asked to add their suggestions. At the meeting the chairman presents all the written suggestions to the group for further additions. Group members then decide which items are to be considered, and in what order.

147

2. At the conclusion of a meeting the chairman asks other members of the group to indicate what problems they consider urgent so that these may be taken up at the next meeting. The problems may have been suggested by written post-meeting reactions or oral comments made at previous meetings. This method of agenda building, although effective in determining priorities, cannot be used successfully unless sufficient time is allowed for it.

3. In some of our larger committees "buzz" groups, or small discussion groups of five or six members, were used successfully to identify specific problems within a large area. After fifteen or twenty minutes the "buzz" group spokesmen report, and the recorder writes the problems on the board. Priorities may then be determined by show of hands. "Buzzing" proved to be an effective and quick way of obtaining agenda proposals in our parent-teacher discussion groups.

4. Polling group members for agenda suggestions prior to meetings, by telephone or in person, serves several purposes. The meeting is called to the attention of group members, interest is developed in advance, and a number of items of business are always suggested.

Relation between understanding of purposes and feelings of satisfaction. Several of our studies yielded relatively convincing evidence of the relation between feelings of satisfaction about a meeting after it had been concluded and the extent to which members had been in agreement about the purpose of the meeting. In investigating this relation, we made use of written, usually anonymous, post-meeting reactions. A representative post-meeting reaction questionnaire is reproduced below.

1. What was the chief purpose of this meeting?
2. What progress did we make in achieving this purpose?
    ( ) Very satisfactory ( ) Satisfactory ( ) So-so
        ( ) Unsatisfactory ( ) Very unsatisfactory

Reactions obtained after our parent-teacher discussion group meetings indicated that there was the widest range in feelings about a meeting—from "Very satisfactory" to "Very unsatisfactory"—when there was the greatest difference of opinion regarding its purpose.

When we did not take sufficient time to discuss and clarify the purposes for which we had presumably come together, many expectations were not met because they had not been expressed. The evaluation "This meeting was a waste of my time because we didn't discuss spelling; I wasn't concerned about problems in teaching literature," which was obtained after an English teachers' workshop, indicates the dissatisfaction likely to be felt when inadequate attention has been given to clarifying purposes and selecting tasks acceptable to the group as a whole.

Relation between cooperative agenda building and member involvement. We found that whatever we did to involve all members actively in the work of the group was well worth the investment of time. Having a hand in deciding just what their group was to do, and how, helped to bring about this involvement. Members assumed greater responsibility for presenting ideas they had gained from background reading, for participating in panels and general discussions, and for working on interim committees when the problems considered were those they had suggested. Willingness to give careful thought to agenda building was, of course, greatly influenced by initial interest in the over-all task of the group.

A group's continued interest in task identification depends on the progress it makes in accomplishing the tasks. As has been emphasized throughout this book, one of the major functions of the status leader is to help a group carry out the tasks identified by it as important. For example, a group of eighth-grade teachers engaged in curriculum planning wanted to improve their use of literary material in connection with units on the American heritage. They agreed that they might benefit most if they observed a series of three demonstration lessons, given by a teacher particularly skillful in using this kind of material, and followed their observations by a half-day conference. The coordinator of instruction was asked by the group to make the necessary arrangements, which involved (1) getting substitute teachers for all members of group; (2) planning with the demonstration teacher; (3) arranging the time and place for the lessons and selecting the student group to be used; (4) planning for the conference; (5) securing the assistance of a consultant from the central office; and (6) planning a method of evaluating the undertaking so that a report could be made to the assistant superintendent of schools. (The report was thought necessary in order to justify the assistant superintendent's authorization of expenditures for substitute teachers and the use of what appeared to be an unusual amount of teacher time.)

Any status leader will at first be tested by a group to see whether or not he is willing and able to provide the means he controls and the group requires. The status leader, for example, is often in the best position to modify schedules, provide clerical and mimeographing services, clear proposed plans with the central office, coordinate the activities of several groups, and clarify the limits within which a group can take action. We found that the work of small groups was always expedited when the status leader was alert to the kinds of help he alone could provide, accepted his responsibilities willingly, and kept his promises.

The Value of Agenda Flexibility

The agenda should be viewed as flexible; the group should feel free to modify it at any point in a meeting. Leaders often become impatient with apparent digressions even though these may channel discussion into important areas. We found that when status leaders or others insisted on adherence to a previously agreed-upon agenda, members lost interest. A group should be reminded that it has departed from its agenda, but the decision to continue or discontinue the present discussion should be made by the group as a whole. Very often we became engrossed in some activity that was interesting but that, when our attention was called to the amount of time we were spending on it, was clearly making little contribution to our major task. Although we often resented reminders that we were digressing, such reminders enabled us to decide intelligently whether or not the digression was worth continuing.

At a meeting of one of our larger committees (twenty-nine members) less than the thirty allotted minutes remained for the final item of business. The chairman asked the group whether it wanted to discuss the item in the time remaining or postpone it until the next meeting. Group members indicated that they wished to place the item on the agenda for the next meeting, thus modifying the original plan. When the chairman asked how the group wanted to use the remaining minutes, one group member proposed an informal discussion of a recent event that concerned everyone. A thoughtful discussion followed, which resulted in group action. It is apparent now that this was the most important business transacted that year. Because the agenda was regarded as flexible by chairman and group members, an area of real concern to all was discovered and constructive action taken.

Meetings: Physical Arrangements, Time Allotment, Opportunities for Acquaintance

In most small working groups someone must accept responsibility for a number of arrangements in connection with meetings—arrangements that often seem, at first, to be routine. Their importance, we found, is much greater than we at first realized.

Physical Arrangements

Attention and time must be devoted to providing comfortable seating accommodations, adequate ventilation and lighting, blackboards and other materials when they are needed, and so on. Time and again we found ourselves in meetings where the chairs were uncomfortable or had been placed so that members could not communicate readily with one another, the atmosphere was stuffy, and no blackboard was available when we needed one for our work.

Often, arranging for the physical well-being of a group is an initial step in increasing group productivity. This does not mean that all arrangements must be made before the group assembles. Sometimes getting a room ready for work is an interesting and easy warm-up activity in which everyone can participate. We found, however, that unless we forced ourselves to think about seating accommodations, lighting, ventilation, and needed materials, we tended to forget about them altogether or follow traditional patterns, which might not be those most conducive to good work.

We were particularly impressed, in connection with seating arrangements, with the importance of the position we as status leaders took in the group. We found that we were more quickly accepted as participant members and facilitators of group work if we did not sit each time in the same place. We were especially careful to stay away from any chair that looked as if it might be the head position.

As improved leadership concepts and practices spread, more and more teachers began to experiment with a circular arrangement of chairs in their classrooms. Some, however, continued to have students arrange their chairs in a circle only when parent-teacher discussion groups planned to use the room. When one group member walked into a classroom whose desks had been left in formal rows, he exclaimed, "What! Are we back to the system where one person tells the others what to do?" The teachers of one school tried out a number of different seating arrangements and discovered that when students are seated so that they face one another, better communication and learning result.

Time Allotment

Face-to-face groups do better work when they are small enough so that everyone can be heard from in the allotted meeting time. Up to a certain maximum, we found that the size of a working group should be determined by the requirements of the job to be done. It was wasteful to have fifteen people spend their time at a task five could do as well, and communication and participation problems usually increased rapidly as group membership exceeded twelve or fifteen. Sometimes, as in the leadership project itself, the nature of our work required a rather large total group; in such a situation we ordinarily found it wise, as our work got under way, to break up into several smaller groups.

Often, written post-meeting reactions indicated that the arrangements that had been made for frequency or duration of meetings should be modified. For example, many members of one of our large PTA groups reported on their post-meeting reaction questionnaires that they wanted longer discussion periods. As a result, meeting time was lengthened from one to one and a half hours. This extension was necessary if groups were to accomplish the tasks they only had time to identify when meetings lasted sixty minutes. Reactions from the same PTA group also indicated the desire of members for more evening meetings so that fathers might join in the discussions and "learn more about their own daughters and sons." Mothers were anxious to share their experiences with fathers and to have them participate in making decisions for their boys and girls. One Denver junior high school scheduled all PTA meetings in the evening, and another is moving in that direction.

We found it difficult at first to estimate how long it would take to complete a job, but analyzing a total task into its components and calculating the length of time required for each helped us to become more realistic and accurate. For example, one committee of five members met to discuss the preparation of an annual progress report. After discussion it was decided that five parts would have to be written. Each of the five members of the committee volunteered to write one part, and one week was allocated for this task. This left one week for reactions from the committee as a whole before the report was to be presented to the East District Articulation Committee. The fact that the time needed for each part of the job had been carefully determined and a deadline set was a powerful stimulus to action.

Whenever possible, committee meetings should be scheduled in advance to avoid conflict with other appointments and responsibilities. The practice of calling meetings on the spur of the moment is not conducive to good feelings or good work. Several Denver schools now prepare a schedule of meetings for an entire semester so that teachers can plan other activities accordingly. It is inevitable that small groups will sometimes find it impossible to arrange dates for meetings in advance, but an effort should always be made to do so.

Opportunities for Acquaintance

The ability of members to communicate freely and clearly with one another is essential to effective group work. Among conditions encouraging the free exchange of ideas and opinions, none is more important than the personal acquaintance and friendship of group members.

At first some of us tended to feel guilty about devoting working time to purely social activities. It took us a while to realize that because we worked more efficiently and cooperatively after we had come to know one another better, the time devoted to getting acquainted was well spent. Our informal conversations over coffee or luncheon built bonds that enabled us to test ideas and express differences of opinion with less fear of hurting others or being hurt by them. Those of our small groups made up of individuals who knew one another only professionally were characterized by less freedom of expression and less relaxation than groups whose members knew one another socially as well as professionally. The difference became particularly marked during discussions of controversial issues. When two people who know each other only professionally take different positions on a professional problem, they are attacking the only thing they know about each other. When the difference of opinion arises between friends, the threat felt by each is much less serious, and it is much easier for each person to express what he really means and how he really feels.

We tried many ways of helping members of groups with which we worked to become better acquainted. We began with the easiest things. One senior high school coordinator arranged to have coffee ready for "breaks" in staff meetings. In other groups arrangements were made to lunch together. Informality was encouraged at all meetings.

One of the largest committees with which we worked included about thirty teachers, each from a different school. Elementary schools and junior and senior high schools were represented, and many of the teachers did not know one another. At the first meeting of a subcommittee of this large group, cake and coffee, served as people arrived, made it easier for them to talk to one another and become at least slightly acquainted. Members of the subcommittee made their own name tags and ten minutes later were ready to prepare an agenda. The agenda was proposed, evaluated, and adopted in less than fifteen minutes. Toward the end of the meeting officers were elected, and the easy and efficient

155

manner in which they were chosen indicated that even the little that had been done to encourage members to become acquainted with one another had been of value. Members of the subcommittee continued to keep in touch with one another between meetings.

When group members know one another well as people, status differences among them are of less consequence. The effect of status differences may be subtle, but we came to believe that influence exercised through status per se is almost invariably a deterrent to productivity. In groups where many opportunities for becoming acquainted are provided, the effect of status differences and the influence exercised on the basis of status alone tend to be reduced. In addition, because everyone feels freer to talk about himself and about the things he likes to do and can do well, the special abilities of individual members are more likely to be discovered.

Methods of Improving Communication

Efforts to improve communication among group members were never a waste of time. We found the following methods effective:

1. Summarizing the discussion at various times during meetings.

2. Clarifying what another group member had said, whenever there seemed to be misunderstanding, by paraphrasing and checking to see whether we had understood correctly. We asked such questions as the following: Did I hear you say—? Then do you mean—? Is that idea the same as—?

3. Providing a common background for discussion by means of role-playing, films, panel discussions, informal reports, or brief problem surveys by resource persons.

4. Reporting regularly on the status of action proposals made at previous meetings.

156

5. Duplicating copies of records (content and process records, post-meeting reactions, summaries, discussion group bulletins, etc.) and distributing them among group members.

These methods are illustrated and described in greater detail in the sections that follow.

Summarizing Discussion

One group leader helped members to summarize by asking, whenever a summary or transition seemed desirable, "What action have we decided to take?" A group member with one conception of action might answer, "None." But someone with a different conception might say, "We decided to retain the present course of study but to request more meetings on method." Through repeated references to the actions implied by discussion, many ideas can be clarified and group members helped to understand one another and their tasks.

If, during a meeting, the recorder is brought into the discussion from time to time to report to the group its accomplishments, his periodic summary will help members understand better what has been said and what remains to be done. Similarly, if the observer reports on process at various times in the course of the meeting, difficulties in communication can be brought to the attention of the group almost as soon as they become apparent, when they are most easily remedied and misunderstandings corrected.

Clarifying Statements

One status leader set herself the task of raising questions and clarifying, or reflecting, the statements of others in her meetings with teachers. She purposely avoided introducing new ideas. These activities helped the group to keep together in its discussion and understand more or less the same thing by what had been said. They also served as a kind of "in-

157

service" training for group members, who in turn began to reflect the feelings and ideas of others and to assume more frequently the roles of questioner and clarifier.

Providing Common Background

The post-meeting reactions from one of nine small parent-teacher discussion groups revealed that all fourteen members had rated the meeting "Very good." An analysis of the procedures used by this group showed that they differed from those of the other eight in that the leader had begun the meeting with a short role-playing episode worked out by a few group members prior to the meeting. The role-playing incident was related to a parent-student problem. The high ratings given the meeting seemed to confirm our hypothesis that an experience common to all group members would make communication among them easier and stimulate discussion.

One group used the film *Shy Guy* as an introduction to a parent-teacher discussion of the topic "Understanding Adolescents." A spirited discussion followed, in which 87 per cent of the members participated orally. Twice as many fathers contributed to the discussion as those participating in previous meetings. Comments explaining the unusually high ratings given this meeting on the post-meeting reaction questionnaires called attention to the improved communication resulting from the provision of an experience common to all group members as a basis for discussion.

Reporting on Action Proposals

Keeping groups informed about what becomes of their recommendations or decisions is essential to continued interest, confidence, and cooperative work. This principle was supported many times in our work with small groups. For example, one of our parent advisory committees proposed that, as an experiment, the traditional mother-daughter,

158

father-son meeting be changed. A short time before a decision on the recommendation had to be made, the proposed change proved unfeasible and was rejected. One staff member suggested that in order to maintain good relations between teachers and parents, the parent committee be informed of this decision and the reasons for it at a special meeting. This suggestion was adopted, and it proved to have been a wise one.

Duplicating Copies of Records

Adequate communication often requires duplicating copies of agenda, minutes, and reports. Written communication helps group members review activities of previous meetings and prepare for the meeting to come. The use of duplicated copies of content records proved to be an economical and effective way of helping members of small teacher planning groups recall action proposals and decisions made at previous meetings. In one school a parent-teacher discussion group bulletin, proposed at a meeting of all discussion group leaders, proved a means of sharing the content and process of each half-grade discussion group's meetings with the other five half-grade discussion groups. This bulletin also provided any group wishing to improve its working procedures with a basis for discussion.

Methods of Increasing Participation

An effort was made in every group—sometimes without much success—to encourage all members to participate whenever they wished to do so. At the beginning, attempts to increase participation met with considerable resistance from a number of people, who insisted that it was possible to benefit from the work of a group without participating actively in it. Although it is true that an individual may derive some benefit in this way, nonparticipation has two serious disadvantages. First, the other members of the group do not have a chance to benefit from the nonparticipant's ideas. Second, the nonparticipant himself does not have a chance to test his ideas against those of other members.

At the beginning of the Denver project we experimented with rather obvious and direct methods of increasing oral participation. We relied almost exclusively on counting the number of times each member contributed to a discussion and reporting this number back to the group. As we gained a better understanding of the reasons for nonparticipation and excessive participation, we developed and used a variety of other methods. Some of these are described in the sections that follow.

Small Discussion Groups

In many groups oral participation increased when small discussion or temporary working groups were formed. We discovered that participation in a total group of twenty, let us say, was appreciably different from and less widespread than that in four subgroups of five each, formed from the same total group.

Questions by Group Leaders

Skillful questioning by a group leader is an effective method of increasing participation. Many different kinds of questions help to involve reticent members. Our records are full of such queries as the following: Are there other suggestions? Do the other members of the subcommittee have additions? Will someone summarize the three suggestions that have been made? Will someone volunteer to find this out for our next meeting? Will you ask two members of the staff to help you work out the plan for evaluation visits? Would anyone like to comment before we go ahead? Jack, don't you think some information about your project would help the group?

160

Training Sessions

Training sessions for group leadership teams result in more widespread participation of group members. In one junior high school, training sessions for leadership teams consisting of a chairman, observer, and recorder were held before each series of parent-teacher discussion group meetings. Some of the methods tried during these training sessions and found effective in subsequent meetings were the following:

1. Having husband-wife teams lead discussions.

2. Having resource committees investigate and report facts in the area to be discussed.

3. Delegating hostess responsibilities to the group member in whose classroom the meeting is to be held.

4. Having one member of the group record important points on the blackboard during a meeting.

5. Engaging in role-playing and panel discussions.

6. Having group members draw slips of paper on which the leadership role or responsibility to be assumed has been written. In one group the roles of chairman, recorder, and observer were rotated periodically in this way.

7. Using volunteering as a means of sharing responsibility in groups.

8. Changing the usual arrangement of chairs in a room.

9. Changing the place of meeting. One meeting was held in the room of a group member who ordinarily did not participate. She enjoyed the role of hostess; her participation in the group's work increased; finally, she volunteered to be a recorder for the following semester.

10. Assigning observation roles to members of the audience during a role-playing situation. ("Watch role-player no. 3. Be ready to discuss why he acted as he did.") This proved an effective way of drawing fathers into the discussion at an 8 B parent-teacher meeting on student behavior.

Polling of Group Members

Group members should sometimes be polled to determine the kinds of activities in which they wish to participate. Polling members to determine their interests and needs enables the leader to draw on resources within the group and gives members an opportunity to indicate the kind of participation they prefer. Some may wish only to learn from others without participating actively; some may wish to share their experiences; some may desire to work in specific ways on specific group tasks.

Analysis of Participation

Oral participation tends to be overemphasized in group work. We learned early in the project that contributing to discussions is not the only form participation, or involvement, can take. Volunteering for jobs to be done, seeing to it that introductions are made, attending closely to what is being said, supporting members of the group who are reticent—all are forms of participation.

As we have said, our analyses of participation were at first limited almost entirely to tabulations of the frequency of oral contributions. Gradually, our interest shifted to quality of participation and reasons for nonparticipation or excessive participation. One of the teacher planning groups tried to make proposals for action and carry out decisions only *after* everyone had participated by commenting or raising questions. Getting reticent members to take part in group discussions seemed to be the first step in bringing about their participation in other areas of group work. Some needed a great deal of encouragement before they were willing to take even this first step.

Questions asked on post-meeting reaction questionnaires helped us to discover the reasons for an individual's belief that he participated too actively or not actively enough.

Responses such as the following, as well as other comments made orally, gave us a great deal of helpful information: "I can't bear to have the spotlight on me. . . . Others know more than I. . . . I can't afford to jeopardize my relations with other members by talking as much as I would like. I think the group resents me." By chatting with a nonparticipating member during a pause in the meeting, the leader was sometimes able either to make him feel more secure or to gain an understanding of factors that made it difficult for him to take part in the group's activity.

After making a number of mistakes, we reached an important generalization regarding oral participation. People rarely *choose* to talk very little or a great deal. They are quiet or garrulous because of certain individual or group factors. Trying by direct methods to draw out the reticent member or stop the constant talker is ineffective. Unless the reasons for excessive participation or nonparticipation are understood and something is done about them, no real changes in behavior are likely to take place.

Forms and Records

All face-to-face working groups need an accurate "group memory." In the Denver project we experimented with various ways of recording minutes in an attempt to develop a form that would prove adequate to our needs. For example, we developed and tried out a form on which the recorder or observer could note separately the content of the meeting and the action decisions reached, the names of persons who would carry out the actions, and any process observations that seemed significant for future meetings. Minutes that made action decisions clearly visible proved especially effective. They were duplicated and circulated shortly after a meeting, and marks were made in the margin of copies sent to persons who had agreed to carry out a group decision.

In addition to experimenting with different ways of recording what had happened at a meeting, we used post-meeting reaction questionnaires to find out how members felt about the meetings themselves. If the leader is skillful, analysis of meetings—either process or content—can move smoothly from an informal, oral evaluation to a more formal, recorded analysis. We found that groups usually accepted later attempts at more formal evaluation when the leader began by asking such questions as the following: Why didn't we accomplish what we set out to do? What was good about this meeting? What wasn't good? If post-meeting reaction questionnaires calling for detailed analysis are introduced too early, they defeat the purposes for which they were intended. Only after the group has had some experience in analyzing its activities is it able to see them in relation to task and process.

Content of Records

In discussion-action groups the agenda, pertinent discussion, action proposals, and names of persons who will carry out the actions should be made a matter of record. At the beginning of the project many of the groups with which we worked thought it unnecessary to record what had happened at a meeting. Later we sometimes recorded more than anyone would read or we could use. It took time and a great deal of experimentation to develop awareness of the practical value of records and skill in recording essential information in the most useful way.

Labeled folders and filing cabinets help to make records of group activity readily accessible for follow-up study. It is well to make several extra copies of all records so that these can be given to new members who may join the group later. We found that as time passed, not only the status leader but other members learned to rely on the folders for a record of specific actions decided on by the group.

164

One of the aims of each of nine parent-teacher discussion groups in one school was to improve the school's curriculum and policies, but the minutes did not state clearly what decisions or plans for action had been made. Eventually a form was developed for recording agenda proposals, decisions, and names of persons who had agreed to take action. Use of this form resulted in constructive and rapid action. At the end of the year, when leaders of parent-teacher discussion groups wished to prepare summaries for all the parents, folders containing the records of decisions and recommendations were easily obtained from the files.

Development of Forms

It is advisable for a group to develop its own forms for recording minutes and obtaining evaluations. We had access to several long post-meeting reaction questionnaires that had been used elsewhere, and these gave us good ideas. However, we found that we were most likely to use data if they came from forms we had developed ourselves. The first evaluation instrument used by some of our parent-teacher discussion groups listed ten points for appraisal, all related to goals that were to have been achieved during the first year of experimentation. When new goals were established for the second year of the study, the parent-teacher planning committee developed a different instrument for evaluating progress.

Use of Records

Unless records of group activity and group reactions to activity are used, interest in them wanes. In one Denver school, prior to the leadership project, the records seldom left the coordinator's files. Now the complete folders are being taken home by group leaders after each meeting.

We found that improvement in group work is most likely to come about when group members themselves analyze

165

their post-meeting reactions and content and process records and make proposals for changes on the basis of these analyses. We learned, in addition, that the best results are achieved when the two kinds of records—records of activity and records of reactions to activity—are used in conjunction with each other.

In one school the analysis of records went through the following stages during the three-year period of the leadership project:

1. Coordinator alone analyzed post-meeting reactions and content and process records before filing them away.

2. Coordinator reported information from content and process records and post-meeting reaction questionnaires to group chairman only.

3. Coordinator and chairman jointly analyzed records.

4. All chairmen, recorders, and observers in school jointly analyzed records.

5. Leaders serving one half-grade jointly tabulated, summarized, and analyzed records.

6. Each group analyzed its own records and, on the basis of the analysis, made proposals for redirecting its activities.

Obstacles to Effective Group Work

Regardless of the kind of work small face-to-face groups are engaged in, certain leadership practices help them accomplish their tasks efficiently and others do not. We would like to call attention here to a number of practices, attitudes, assumptions, and omissions on the part of group leaders that, unless modified, constitute obstacles to effective group work.

1. Overlooking the necessity for a realistic appraisal of time required and time available. Our frustrations and mistakes in the leadership project were, for the most part, related to timing. Task identification without consideration

of the time needed to accomplish the task leads to almost insurmountable obstacles to group growth and productivity.

2. Assuming that the quickest way to get action is necessarily the best way. Passive assent to proposals whose real meanings and implications have not been explored by the group plays little part in changing the behavior of group members. It takes time to achieve effective communication and widespread participation, but the results justify this expenditure of time.

3. Using terms that are not understood. This practice usually impedes progress. It is sometimes perceived as a flaunting of knowledge or as a way of manifesting superiority.

4. Talking democratically but using status to influence decisions. A group is quick to recognize this kind of inconsistency. If a leader is really a group member and welcomes, values, and applies suggestions for improving "our" group, whatever shortcomings he may have as a democratic leader can be overlooked. However, if he uses his status in order to force his decisions on the group, it becomes clear that there is a real dichotomy between the democratic leadership he advocates and the kind of leadership he exercises.

5. Failing to help members learn that group success is as much the responsibility of members as it is that of leaders. Groups, like individuals, learn to do by doing. They need opportunities (1) to become sensitive to elements of effective group process through discussion of how they have worked and can work to achieve their goals and (2) to develop skill in assuming responsibility for the success of meetings.

6. Forgetting or ignoring, because of inadequate records, significant group achievements, decisions, action proposals, and suggestions for improvement.

7. Using the group to satisfy personal wishes or ambitions while pretending to be sincerely interested in helping it select goals of significance to its members.

167

8

AN EVALUATION OF
THE LEADERSHIP PROJECT

In October, 1951, the entire Denver group responded anonymously to a number of inventories designed to obtain some relatively objective evidence of what had happened as a result of two and a half years of work. In this chapter each inventory is briefly described; the directions and some or all of the items are reproduced; and an analysis of the responses is presented. Our expectations regarding the leadership project are considered first; then, the various activities in which we engaged, our general achievements, the changes in our leadership practices, and the changes in concepts and beliefs related to leadership. Finally, the mistakes we believe we made are discussed.

Group Expectations

The most valid way of determining the expectations members of a group have regarding the outcomes of a project is to ask for these expectations before the project is begun. During the early months of the Denver study we devoted a

168

great deal of time to formulating purposes and describing goals, but we did not record systematically the significance each of these had for individual participants because we did not then realize the importance of such a record. The data we obtained therefore came from an inventory administered at the conclusion of the project. This inventory, which is reproduced here in its entirety, asked the respondents to recall their expectations at the beginning of the leadership study. Following each item are the mean response and the item's rank in importance.

WHAT EXPECTATIONS DID YOU HAVE CONCERNING THE LEADERSHIP PROJECT?

The items in this inventory are based on statements made by various participants in the leadership project at the May 8, 1951, evaluation session. Each participant is being asked to respond to these items in order that the entire group may know the extent to which there is agreement on the various ideas expressed. Indicate the importance you attach to the expectations listed below by responding to each item according to the following key:

3. For me, this was a very important expectation.
2. For me, this was a moderately important expectation.
1. For me, this was a relatively unimportant expectation.
0. For me, this was not an expectation.

Mark 3, 2, 1, or 0		Mean Response	Rank
——	1. To develop security for a new kind of leadership—that is, for working with adults after working with children	2.3	8
——	2. To learn how to work more effectively with committees, to accept their decisions, and to keep faith with them	2.7	4
——	3. To learn criteria and techniques for good leadership and to practice good leadership	2.9	1

169

EVALUATION OF LEADERSHIP PROJECT

Mark 3, 2, 1, or 0		Mean Response	Rank
——	4. To find out what people really want	2.3	9
——	5. To learn a clear-cut set of leadership procedures and skills	2.2	10.5
——	6. To develop and exercise leadership in our own schools, in groups and with individuals	2.9	2
——	7. To learn how to achieve results without using either an authoritarian or a laissez-faire approach	2.4	7
——	8. To learn how to promote job satisfaction and reduce irritating situations	2.8	3
——	9. To learn why people behave as they do	2.2	10.5
——	10. To learn how to communicate more effectively	2.4	5.5
——	11. To help spread effective leadership techniques to all groups in which we become members	2.4	5.5

As is indicated in the Mean Response column, when the responses of all participants were averaged, each expectation was recalled as having been at least "moderately important" when the project began. The fact that items 3, 6, and 7 ranked first, second, and third in importance indicates that our expectations, as we recalled them, were primarily practical. The relatively low rank of item 5 implies that learning a set group of leadership procedures and skills was not an important expectation. The responses to item 9 indicate that we did not recall having had a very strong desire to find out "why people behave as they do."

170

As we have said in several of the earlier chapters, five different groups participated in the project—junior high school principals, junior high school coordinators, senior high school principals, senior high school coordinators, and central office personnel. There were substantial differences in expectation among these groups. Table 1 shows the percentage of each group recalling various items as representing "very important" expectations.[1]

The size of these groups makes the interpretation of percentages hazardous. Still, it is interesting to note that item 1 was considered to be of great importance by all of the junior high school coordinators, by many of the senior high school coordinators, by half of the junior high school principals, but by none of the senior high school principals. The differences in expectation among participating groups, illustrated by Table 1, are indicative of the heterogeneity of the total group.

We were interested in the number of expectations recalled as "very important" by individual participants. Five people responded to every item with a 3; one person responded to only four items with a 3. There were no sizable differences among the five participating groups in the number of expectations recalled as "very important," but the junior high school coordinators and the central office personnel expected most and the junior high school principals least.

Before discussing the data relating to general achievements (see p. 174–179), we would like to comment briefly on the relation between recalled expectations and reported achievements. When a coefficient of correlation was computed between the two variables—number of recalled ex-

---

[1] The following initials are used in extract and tabular matter to identify participating groups:

JHC—junior high school coordinators
SHC—senior high school coordinators
JHP—junior high school principals
SHP—senior high school principals
COP—central office personnel

171

TABLE 1

PERCENTAGE OF EACH PARTICIPATING GROUP RESPONDING
"VERY IMPORTANT" TO EACH EXPECTATION

Expectation	Percentage of				
	JHC (N=10)	SHC (N=5)	JHP (N=8)	SHP (N=4)	COP (N=8)
1. To develop security for a new kind of leadership— that is, for working with adults after working with children	100	60	50	0	50
2. To learn how to work more effectively with committees, to accept their decisions, and to keep faith with them	90	80	38	100	75
3. To learn criteria and techniques for good leadership and to practice good leadership	90	100	88	100	88
4. To find out what people really want	50	20	25	50	75
5. To learn a clear-cut set of leadership procedures and skills	60	40	63	75	38
6. To develop and exercise leadership in our own schools, in groups and with individuals	100	80	75	100	88
7. To learn how to achieve results without using either an authoritarian or a laissez-faire approach	50	60	38	0	100
8. To learn how to promote job satisfaction and reduce irritating situations	90	80	63	100	88
9. To learn why people behave as they do	50	20	25	25	88
10. To learn how to communicate more effectively	60	40	38	50	75
11. To help spread effective leadership techniques to all groups in which we become members	40	80	63	25	75

pectations and number of reported achievements—an index of .51 was obtained. This does not mean that the relation was close; however, it was not negligible. Those members of the group who recalled having had the greatest number of expectations also tended to believe that they had benefited most from the project.

Learning Activities

During the two and a half years of our work together we engaged in many different kinds of activities. Seventeen major activities were listed on a form used during the October, 1951, evaluation sessions, and each member of the group was asked to indicate for each activity (1) whether or not he had participated in it and (2) his estimate of its value. (A 5-point scale, with 5 indicating "Very worth while" and 1 "Of little or no value," was used.)

Table 2, in which the number of people taking part in each activity and the mean value assigned to it are noted, summarizes the results of our inquiry regarding the relative worth of various activities.

About half of the activities were considered "Worth while" (mean rating, 4 or higher), and only one received a mean rating below 3 ("So-so"). By groups, the average number of activities engaged in was greatest for the junior high school coordinators (10.2) and least for the central office personnel (5.6). Of all the activities in which most members of the group engaged, experimenting on the job was considered most valuable. This again indicates our practical interests. The least valuable activities of those engaged in by a substantial fraction of the total group were interpretation of research data and role-playing. The ratings given the three subgroups that lasted for the first six months of the leadership project invite speculation. The groups were differently organized and attacked different problems. One of them,

173

TABLE 2

ACTIVITIES: NUMBER PARTICIPATING, INDEX OF VALUE, AND RANK

Kind of Activity	Number Participating	Index of Value	Rank
1. Large group meetings	29	4.27	4.5
2. Subgroups			
I: Leadership in In-Service Education	6	3.83	12
II: Group Process	7	4.86	1
III: Leadership Procedures	6	2.67	17
3. Interim groups			
Leadership Practices	23	3.85	11
Interpretation of Data	18	3.33	16
School-Community Relations	8	3.63	14
4. Steering Committee	7	3.71	13
5. Leadership Techniques Committee	5	4.40	3
6. 1950 Workshop	15	3.86	10
7. Building team projects	22	3.91	9
8. Reading	27	4.26	6
9. Role-playing	20	3.45	15
10. Experimenting on the job	25	4.52	2
11. Writing reports of projects	9	4.00	8
12. Conferring with consultants	22	4.27	4.5
13. Corresponding with consultants	14	4.14	7

Subgroup II, was considered by its members to have provided the most valuable experience of the entire project. Subgroup III, on the other hand, was judged to have been the least rewarding of all the activities its members engaged in.

General Achievements

The best way of determining the general or specific achievements resulting from many months of work is to compare data obtained at the beginning and end of the project. Because we were insufficiently interested in "bench mark" information to get any when the project was initiated,

174

we are unable to present this kind of comparison here. Toward the end of the project most of us were asking, How much have we actually learned? But this interest developed too late to enable us to obtain the kind of data yielding the most adequate answer; we were forced to depend on recollections. This kind of situation—realization of the importance of certain data after the opportunity for obtaining them has passed—frequently arises in action research. Our resolution of the particular problem we faced was to obtain the best data we could at the time the hypotheses we were trying to test were seen to be important.

At a spring, 1951, preliminary evaluation meeting, which a number of us attended, some time was devoted to identifying the general achievements resulting from the leadership project. These achievements were summarized after considerable discussion by small and large groups. At that time we made no attempt to determine how many of us considered the various accomplishments important, and to what degree. For the October, 1951, evaluation sessions, the achievements identified were incorporated into an inventory consisting of twenty-seven items. It is reproduced here in its entirety, and after each item are listed the mean response, the item's rank in importance, and the participating group by which the item was considered most important. Asterisks have been placed in front of the six items representing the most significant achievements.

What Are the Achievements Resulting from the Leadership Project?

Indicate what you believe you have achieved in the leadership project by marking the following statements in the left-hand column according to the following key:

        3. A very important achievement
        2. A moderately important achievement
        1. A slightly important achievement
        0. Not achieved at all

Mark 3, 2, 1, or 0		Mean Response	Rank	Group Considering Item Most Important
——	*1. I have been alerted to the value of planning agenda cooperatively.	2.4	4	SHP
——	*2. I have become more sensitive to the importance of using leaders other than status leaders in groups.	2.5	2	SHP
——	3. I have become aware of the importance of evaluating group meetings.	2.2	9	JHC
——	*4. I have come to recognize the value of recording and following up action proposals.	2.5	2	JHC
——	5. I have been alerted to possibilities in the development and use of special forms for recording action proposals.	1.5	27	JHC
——	*6. I have discovered many new ways of working.	2.3	5.5	JHC
——	*7. I have come to recognize that time is necessary for changing behavior, and am less impatient with discussion.	2.3	5.5	JHC-COP
——	8. I have changed my conception of leadership.	2.2	9	SHP
——	9. I have developed greater objectivity.	2.0	18	COP
——	10. I have discovered the importance of getting people to express their views.	1.9	22	COP

176

Mark 3, 2, 1, or 0		Mean Response	Rank	Group Considering Item Most Important
——	11. I have come to realize the importance of establishing a "bench mark."	2.1	13.5	JHC
——	12. I have discovered the importance of evaluative data and have experimented with different ways of getting such data.	1.9	22	JHP-COP
——	13. I have learned some techniques of action research.	2.1	13.5	JHP
——	14. I have learned some techniques of group process and have practiced the roles of recorder and observer.	2.0	18	SHP
——	15. I have become aware of my co-workers as people.	2.0	18	COP
——	16. I have learned to accept the fact that we cannot always realize our goals.	2.2	9	SHP-COP
——	17. I have learned how to work more effectively in the community and have become aware of the importance of keeping the community informed about and interested in the school's work.	1.6	26	JHC
——	18. I have learned the importance of timing and have come to recognize the importance of seeking understanding and support from the faculty.	2.1	13.5	SHC

177

Mark 3, 2, 1, or 0		Mean Response	Rank	Group Considering Item Most Important
——	19. I have discovered that one can use research methods in solving instructional problems.	2.0	18	SHP
——	20. I have become more analytical.	2.0	18	SHC
——	21. Discussions held by groups with which I have worked have improved as a result of the direction I have been able to give.	2.1	13.5	SHP
——	22. Individuals with whom I work come to me more frequently for assistance with problems.	1.9	22	JHC-SHC
——	23. I have become more critical of process. I am better able to recognize successful group work and understand why some groups are more successful than others.	1.8	24	JHC
——	24. I have met recent criticisms and attacks more effectively because of our emphasis on group process.	2.2	9	SHP-COP
——*25.	We have become better acquainted as persons.	2.5	2	COP
——	26. The job satisfaction of teachers with whom I work has noticeably increased.	1.7	25	JHC

178

EVALUATION OF LEADERSHIP PROJECT

Mark 3, 2, 1, or 0		Mean Response	Rank	Group Considering Item Most Important
—— 27.	I have learned some methods of encouraging reticent members to participate in meetings.	2.2	9	SHC

As has been said, asterisks have been placed in front of the six items representing the most significant achievements. Five of the six (items 1, 2, 4, 6, and 7) are related to improvements in group process. One (item 25) indicates that the project helped us to become better acquainted with one another and that this was important to us. Of the five participating groups, the junior high school coordinators reported the greatest number of achievements. The other groups followed in this order: senior high school principals, with central office personnel reporting about the same number; senior high school coordinators; and junior high school principals.

There were great individual differences in reported achievement. The mean score for all items for the thirty-four people who responded to this inventory ranged from 2.93 to 1.00, with a median of 2.11. In other words, one person felt that all except two items represented "very important" achievements. At the other extreme, one individual considered none of the items to represent more than a "slightly important" achievement.

Changes in Leadership Practices

One of the committees active during the first two years of the project compiled a list of practices, beliefs, and concepts considered by all of us to be related to good instructional leadership. One of the purposes of this activity was to bring together the learnings of the group, and the list went through several revisions. Desirable practices and the concepts and beliefs on which they were based were suggested to the committee at different times. The suggestions were then mimeographed, and their relative importance was checked by several of us. In its final stages the list was edited by members of the Institute staff. Some of the items were reworded to clarify their meaning, duplications were eliminated, and items were classified under ten major headings.

This list was the basis for an inventory administered in two parts in October, 1951. Part I was entitled "Leadership Practices," and included sixty-five items. The first page of this section of the evaluation instrument is reproduced below.

Part I: Leadership Practices

This is a final revision of several instruments and other types of materials which you have helped the Leadership Techniques Committee develop. What we are trying to do is to get some evidence concerning leadership practices in 1948, before the project started, and in 1951, as it closes. This evidence will certainly be fallible because we did not get "bench mark" data in 1948. But it will be better than no evidence at all. We are asking you to do your best to *recall* your practices of 1948. Responses in the left-hand column are to describe your practices *now*. The right-hand column is for your recollections—as objective as possible—of your practices *in 1948*.

Please place a number in the parentheses according to the following key to indicate whether you engage (1951—Column I) or engaged (1948—Column II) in the practice named:

1. Always or almost always
2. Frequently
3. Sometimes
4. Rarely
5. Never

Column I　　　　　　　　　　　　　　*Column II*
1951　　　　　　　　　　　　　　　　1948

A. *Planning and Preparing for Group Meetings*

(　) 1. Provide considerable leeway to the group　(　)
in choosing meeting times and places

(　) 2. Permit the group to determine whether　(　)
attendance at meetings shall be optional
or required

(　) 3. Prepare notices with a tentative agenda　(　)
and encourage group members to make
additions or deletions

(　) 4. Plan with a steering committee ways of　(　)
helping larger groups move ahead more
easily

(　) 5. Conduct preliminary meetings to identify　(　)
problems as group members see them

The nature of this inventory makes clear that any quantitative indices of change are based on our recollections of the practices we engaged in at the beginning of the study (1948) and our reports of our practices at its end (1951). We have already expressed our awareness of the inadequacy of data such as these for measuring growth. Evidence of change that consists of recollections, however, need not be misleading if its nature is taken into consideration when interpretations are made. Our reactions represent our perceptions of what we did before and what we do now. No attempt was made to check these perceptions against "reality"— against our actual practices. This would have been difficult to do, and we did not think it important. We were primarily interested, at the time, in ascertaining what we *believed* the benefits of the study to be.

As has been said, the "Leadership Practices" section of the inventory included sixty-five items, organized under such headings as Planning and Preparing for Group Meetings,

181

Encouraging Participation, Sharing Leadership with Group Members, Improving Human Relations. All the items were phrased in such a way as to represent practices we considered desirable. Had anyone responded to all the items with a 1, indicating that he "Always or almost always" engaged in this practice, his total score would have been 65.00, and his mean score, 1.00. At the other extreme, the individual who reported that he "Never" engaged in any of the practices would have received a total score of 325.00 and a mean score of 5.00.

We were interested in the reliability of this part of the inventory—in whether or not it would rank individuals in the group with some degree of stability. Consequently, we computed a split-half reliability coefficient, which, after correction by the Spearman-Brown formula, resulted in an index of .88. We interpreted this to mean that the items differentiated among members of the group with a relatively high degree of dependability.

Average Reported Change

We took the following steps to make the data obtained easier to handle: (1) The responses of each person to each item were recorded on a master data sheet. (2) The mean of the thirty-four responses to each item was computed separately for the "1948" and "1951" columns. (3) The difference between the "1948" and "1951" mean responses to each item was computed. (4) The average of these means was computed (*a*) for Part I as a whole and (*b*) for sections of Part I. (5) The "1948" and "1951" mean scores of each individual were computed. (6) The difference between the "1948" and "1951" mean scores was computed (*a*) for each individual and (*b*) for each participating group.

Our method of summarizing responses is illustrated in Table 3 for items C-6 ("Credit originators when repeating their ideas") and D-1 ("Provide members with summaries

TABLE 3

RESPONSES TO ITEMS C-6 AND D-1

Individual	Item C-6		Item D-1	
	1948	1951	1948	1951
1	4	2	5	1
2	1	1	1	1
3	1	1	4	2
4	2	1	2	1
5	1	1	3	1
6	1	1	1	1
7	1	1	5	1
8	2	1	3	2
9	2	2	4	2
10	1	1	3	1
11	1	1	1	1
12	1	1	2	1
13	1	1	2	1
14	2	1	4	2
15	1	1	3	2
16	2	1	4	1
17	2	1	4	3
18	1	1	4	3
19	1	1	2	2
20	1	1	4	3
21	1	1	1	1
22	2	2	3	2
23	2	1	4	2
24	2	2	3	2
25	1	1	4	2
26	1	1	2	1
27	1	1	4	3
28	2	2	2	2
29	2	2	4	3
30	1	1	1	1
31	1	1	2	2
32	1	1	4	1
33	3	1	4	2
34	3	1	2	2
Mean	1.59	1.18	2.97	1.71
Difference		.41		1.26

of previous meetings, agenda for next meeting, and other materials to help move group work ahead").

The mean "1948" response to item C-6 was 1.59. The mean "1951" response to this same item was 1.18, and the difference between the two mean scores, .41. In other words, the practice represented by item C-6 was reported, on the average, to be slightly more common in 1951 than in 1948. For item D-1 the reported change—1.26—was three times as great as that for item C-6.

We predicted that the average reported change for all items—that is, for Part I as a whole—would be appreciable because the major emphasis throughout the project had been on *doing* things differently. Reading and talking about improvements in leadership were consistently subordinated to actually trying out promising new practices and studying their consequences.

The median of the differences between averaged "1948" and "1951" responses to each item was .84, and the mean of these differences, .83. It is, we recognize, difficult to interpret the significance of a change represented by an index of this size. The maximum difference possible, given the scoring method used, is 4.00. This represents a reported change from "Never" to "Always or almost always" for each of the items. The obtained median difference of .84 is 21 per cent of the change possible to report. This seemed to us to represent significant change, especially in view of the fact that many of the items described practices that had received only incidental attention throughout the project. The range in average change—considering the sixty-five items separately—was from 10 per cent to 35 per cent of the amount possible to report.

We identified the thirteen items for which the greatest change was reported and the thirteen for which the least was reported. For all items for which the greatest change was reported, the difference between averaged "1948" and

"1951" responses was in excess of 1.03, or at least 26 per cent of the change possible to report. For those items for which the least change was reported, the difference between the averaged "1948" and "1951" responses was .6 or less—no more than 15 per cent of the change possible to report.

The following are the thirteen items for which the greatest change was reported:

1. Prepare notices with a tentative agenda and encourage group members to make additions or deletions
2. Plan with a steering committee ways of helping larger groups move ahead more easily
3. Conduct preliminary meetings to identify problems as group members see them
4. Canvass group members at the beginning of the meeting for additions or revisions to a previously planned agenda
5. Clarify commitments and agreements, list problems, plan agenda, etc., using a blackboard or other help
6. Provide members with summaries of previous meetings, agenda for next meeting, and other materials to help move group work ahead
7. Use "buzz" sessions and other involvement techniques
8. Permit final determination of action to be made by the new leader, limiting advice to pointing out variety of possible actions, decisions, results, etc.
9. Allow the new chairman to assume full responsibility; avoid too early "rescue" when difficulties are encountered
10. Prepare and use content and process forms
11. Use data obtained as a basis for planning next step
12. Ascertain what comments were made in the "buzz" sessions
13. Provide opportunity for the group to consider the matter of timing in relation to suggested problems

Most of these practices represent improvements in group process—cooperative agenda building, sharing leadership responsibilities, and obtaining post-meeting reactions. As we have said in some of the earlier chapters, there was a constant emphasis, throughout the project, on improving meth-

185

ods of group work. It is true, also, that many of the practices that were reported to have changed most involved fairly specific activities (items 1, 4, 5, 6, 7, 10, and 13). When concrete ways of improving leadership were called to our attention, we were able to incorporate them in our behavior in a relatively short time.

The thirteen items for which the least change was reported are listed below. Asterisks have been placed in front of those items—eight—describing practices recalled as having been frequently employed in 1948.

1. Permit individual members to choose the group in which each wishes to participate
2. Prevent the same people from doing either "too much" or "everything"
*3. Begin and end the meetings on time
*4. Credit originators when repeating their ideas
*5. Participate courteously in all discussions
*6. Express personal opinions freely when asked to do so
7. Use common terms, define carefully any new terms used, and avoid "pedaguese"
8. Direct specific questions to members to get them to participate
*9. Use all contributions, if possible
10. Seek contributions in specific ways from individuals according to their abilities
*11. Give special recognition to good work or significant contributions
*12. Provide suggestions to keep discussion moving when it appears the group is bogging down
*13. Commend freely when there is a basis for commendation

As has been said, eight of these items describe practices recalled as having been frequently employed in 1948—practices in which, therefore, little improvement was possible. If evaluating the consequences of a group meeting is considered a desirable leadership practice, and if this was done rarely in 1948, improvement might be expected during the course of the project. If, however, starting and closing meetings on time is also considered a good leadership practice but was very common in 1948, little change can be expected. The hypothesis implied by these two illustrations was supported by our data. The coefficient of correlation between reported frequency of practices in 1948 and amount of change inferred from comparing "1948" and "1951" responses was −.65.

Differences among Individuals and Groups

We averaged each person's "1948" and "1951" responses and obtained the difference between the two averages. The distribution of these differences exhibited a marked degree of positive skewness—the mean was .83 and the median .69. The latter figure, which indicates more accurately the tendency of the group, represents a reported change approximately 17 per cent of that possible to report.

Whether this reported change can be called significant is questionable. Individual differences were great, responses ranging from 4 to 70 per cent of the change possible to report. The greatest mean change was reported by the junior high school coordinators (1.04); and the least, by members of the central office staff (.65). This was anticipated because the latter group—for a number of reasons—was not as deeply involved in project activities as the others. The mean number of activities engaged in by the junior high school coordinators was 10.2. The mean number engaged in by members of the central office staff was 5.6 (see p. 173).

Changes in Leadership Concepts and Beliefs

The second part of the inventory discussed in the preceding section was designed to obtain data concerning changes in beliefs and concepts related to instructional leadership. The items for this part of the inventory resulted from

187

the work of the same committee that had prepared the list of desirable leadership practices and were derived from the thinking and deliberations of the total group. The first page of this part of the inventory is reproduced below.

PART II: CONCEPTS AND BELIEFS

Again using the two columns to indicate your beliefs now (1951) and then (1948), please place a number in the parentheses according to the following key:

1. Accept the generalization completely
2. Accept the generalization with a few reservations
3. Am uncertain; haven't reached a conclusion
4. Have quite a bit of doubt regarding the truth of the generalization
5. Reject the generalization as substantially untrue

Column I   *Column II*
1951   *1948*

A. Planning and Preparing for Group Meetings

( ) 1. The leader should plan *with* the group ( )
       rather than for the group.

( ) 2. The agenda should be planned coopera- ( )
       tively in order to select problems which
       are both real and significant to the mem-
       bers of the group.

B. Selecting Group Members

( ) 1. Group membership should be studied ( )
       critically and carefully in order to secure
       "balanced" groups.

Part II of the inventory included forty-six items, organized under such headings as Planning and Preparing for Group Meetings, Selecting Group Members, Facilitating Communication, Evaluating Group Meetings. All the items were phrased in such a way as to represent beliefs and concepts we considered desirable. The method of scoring Part II was similar to that used to score Part I (see p. 182). The reliability coefficient for Part II was .90.

Average Reported Change

We predicted, for two reasons, that no substantial change in beliefs and concepts related to instructional leadership would be reported. First, many of us had thought about and discussed leadership for many years prior to the cooperative study. From the beginning of the project we were fairly well satisfied with our ideas about and attitudes toward instructional leadership. Most of our dissatisfaction had to do with the extent to which we could put these concepts and beliefs into practice.

The second reason for making this prediction was the great difficulty of recalling beliefs and concepts held two and a half years earlier and different from those held at the time the inventory was administered. It is much more difficult to recall "different" beliefs and concepts operative two and a half years ago than it is to recall "different" practices actually engaged in two and a half years ago.

The data we obtained seemed to support our prediction. The "1948" median score for all concept-belief items— that is, for Part II as a whole—was 1.67. This means that the reported acceptance of the typical item in 1948 fell between the following response possibilities:

1. Accept the generalization completely
2. Accept the generalization with a few reservations

The "1951" median score for all concept-belief items was 1.20. The difference between the "1948" and the "1951" median scores was .47. The change reported was therefore approximately 12 per cent of the change possible to report with the scoring method employed. The reader will recall

189

that the reported change in practices was 21 per cent of that possible to report.

The nine concept-belief items for which the greatest change was reported are listed below. As is true of the leadership practices in which the greatest change was reported to have occurred, most of these concepts and beliefs relate to methods of group work.

1. The agenda should be planned cooperatively in order to select problems which are both real and significant to the members of the group.
2. Planning should proceed no faster than group members can or are willing to proceed.
3. Leadership should pass from one group member to another.
4. Meetings can be improved by determining group feelings about the session and securing suggestions for change.
5. The leader should direct the attention of the group to process as well as content.
6. The leader should improve the efficiency of group activity by directing attention to mechanics that can help.
7. The leader should work consciously to perfect group processes and techniques.
8. All progress may be lost by impatience and pushing on the part of the leader.
9. The leader is only one member of the group.

The nine items for which the least change was reported are listed below. Asterisks have been placed in front of those items—seven—that were in the top fifth of the distribution so far as reported acceptance in 1948 was concerned, and for which little change in acceptance was, therefore, possible.

*1. The suggestions of all members of the group should be recognized fairly.
*2. The leader should not give the group the impression of either "knowing it all" or "knowing nothing at all."
*3. Individual potentialities should be discovered and utilized.
 4. Opportunities for accepting greater responsibility should be provided those who have indicated a willingness to accept it.

*5. The worth of each individual must be recognized.

*6. Individuals should feel free to confer with the leader at any time.

*7. The leader should feel responsible for meeting appointments promptly and preparing for these as adequately as possible.

*8. Job satisfaction is important for good mental health and professional success.

9. Help should be provided individual group members at the earliest opportunity if it is needed or requested.

Differences among Individuals

The difference between averaged "1948" responses and averaged "1951" responses was calculated for each individual. The mean of the thirty-three differences was .49; the median, .45. Two persons reported the greatest modification in beliefs and concepts—35 per cent of the change possible to report with the scoring method used. Seven reported the least modification—2 per cent of the change possible to report. The difference between these two extremes impressed us as being very great and called attention again to the tremendous variation in reported benefit from the project.

Relation between Reported Change in Concepts and Beliefs and Reported Change in Practices

As we have said, the reported change in beliefs and concepts was appreciably less than the reported change in practices. We were interested in finding out whether or not those individuals who recalled having changed their beliefs and concepts most also recalled having changed their practices most. One method of ascertaining to what degree such a relation exists is to rank all members of the group on the basis of their mean reported change in concepts and beliefs, rank them again on the basis of their mean reported change in practices, and then compute a coefficient of correlation between the two rankings.

191

When we subjected our scores to this kind of statistical analysis, we obtained a correlation coefficient of .56. This index indicates that although there was a definite relation between the two variables, it was not close. One way of clarifying the significance of the correlation coefficient is to say that the average difference in rank between the two distributions was 6.7, with 33 ranks involved. In other words, the typical individual ranked in entirely different fifths of the two distributions. Another way of saying the same thing is that 31 per cent of the individuals were on different sides of the median in the two distributions.

Even though no great change in beliefs and concepts was reported for the two-and-a-half-year period, we thought that the correlation between "1951" concept-belief and practice scores would be higher than that between "1948" concept-belief and practice scores. In other words, the tendency for those individuals with better concept-belief scores to have better practice scores would be greater in 1951 than it had been in 1948.

A correlation analysis of the "1948" and "1951" scores supported our hypothesis. The coefficient of correlation between "1948" concept-belief and practice scores for the thirty-three individuals involved was .56. The correlation between "1951" concept-belief and practice scores was .57. The latter index, however, was appreciably affected by the greater homogeneity of both "1951" scores. The standard deviations are given in Table 4.

TABLE 4

STANDARD DEVIATIONS OF "1948" AND "1951"
PRACTICE AND CONCEPT-BELIEF SCORES

Score	Standard Deviation	
	1948	1951
Practice	.56	.32
Concept-Belief	.58	.25

The effect of homogeneity is to lower the coefficient of correlation. If the coefficient of correlation between "1951" practice and concept-belief scores had been derived from a distribution as heterogeneous as that of the "1948" scores, its value would have increased from .57 to .88.

Our Mistakes

The last evaluation instrument used in October, 1951, was a forty-eight-item inventory developed to ascertain the feelings of the group about mistakes that might have been made in the leadership project. The directions for this inventory and a few sample items are given below.

WHAT MISTAKES DID WE MAKE, AND WHAT SHORTCOMINGS OR DEFICIENCIES DID THE STUDY HAVE?

As you view the leadership project in retrospect, indicate your opinion about it by responding to each item according to the following key:

        3. A very significant deficiency
        2. A moderately significant deficiency
        1. A slightly significant deficiency
        0. Not a significant deficiency

—— 1. Project lacked a sense of direction, a coordinated plan, and clear-cut objectives.

—— 2. The team idea left out many individuals.

—— 3. It moved very slowly.

—— 4. Many decisions were made because we felt we should grab at something.

—— 5. The leaders let us flounder too long.

—— 6. Time pressures kept teams from functioning as teams.

The items for this inventory resulted from a more informal evaluation that had taken place during the previous spring.

193

At that time "free responses" had been made to a request that major limitations of the study be described. These were combined, and duplications eliminated, for the inventory used in October. The split-half reliability coefficient for this inventory was .87, which represents substantial stability of response. Not only did the inventory differentiate among individuals who responded to it, but the responses individuals made to the various items were sufficiently different to imply discrimination.

The nine items representing the most serious difficulties faced during the project are listed below. They are ranked in order of their seriousness. The weight of each item, as indicated by the average of all responses to it, is given in parentheses.

1. Members did not realize the amount of time necessary for getting the most out of such a study. They did not prepare adequately for each visit of the consultants. (2.6)
2. Time pressures kept teams from functioning as teams. (2.3)
3. The pressure of time has continued to be an irritant, if not an actual detriment to our study. (2.3)
4. Certain resistances to the project were not analyzed and therefore could not be dealt with adequately. (2.0)
5. Insufficient time was spent at the beginning in exploring the possibilities of the study. As a result, a basis for unity and sound problem definition was not developed. (1.9)
6. Many of the group were not interested in an action research approach to the learning of leadership techniques. (1.9)
7. Many decisions were made because we felt we should grab at something. (1.9)
8. Project lacked a sense of direction, a coordinated plan, and clear-cut objectives. (1.8)
9. At times we were up in the clouds. (1.8)

The responses to four, or about half, of these items (1, 2, 3, and 5) reflected our feeling that we had had insufficient time to devote to the project. There were a number of reasons for time pressures. Everyone involved in the leader-

194

ship study also carried on his regular work. Because we did not realize how much work and time various team projects would require, some commitments were made that proved impossible to meet. This naturally resulted in anxiety and frustration.

Item 4, which refers to the unanalyzed "resistances" to the project, is ambiguous because it does not state explicitly in what areas resistance developed or what was resisted. Item 6 suggests that one of the activities to which resistance developed was the action research approach to improvement of leadership practices. The procedures of action research— defining problems, hypothesizing, putting the hypothesis into action, obtaining evidence concerning consequences, and formulating generalizations based on the evidence— were strange to us at first. As we reported in Chapter 4, obtaining objective evidence was especially difficult. There is reason to believe, however, from the responses to the inventory designed to investigate changes in beliefs and practices, that continued experience with action research led to increased confidence in it as a learning methodology.

It is true that we gave insufficient attention, at the beginning of the project, to difficulties that might well have been anticipated. Many of us had unrealistic expectations regarding the immediate consequences of a leadership training program. A better understanding of how changes in behavior come about, and how quickly, would have tended to correct these expectations. Research projects, too, were often begun in an unrealistically optimistic fashion, without clear realization of what might be involved. The fact that this difficulty, though recognized verbally, was not overcome was viewed by the consultants as a shortcoming of theirs. They were learning, too.

The shortcomings identified in items 7 and 8 are probably related. We found it difficult to see the relation of different building team projects to one another and spent too little

195

time, during meetings of the total group, in trying to discover and accentuate this interrelatedness. As a result, individual teams tended to feel that they were working without the necessary understanding and support of the group as a whole. The one element most of our projects clearly had in common was their emphasis on human relations problems. This fact may explain why the greatest reported changes, in beliefs as well as practices, occurred in the area of group work.

The nine items that seemed to members of the group to represent the least significant shortcomings are listed below. The item with the lowest rank—the shortcoming of least significance—appears first, and the others are listed in sequence. The mean response to each item is again given in parentheses.

1. Status differences between junior and senior high school leaders impeded the progress of the total group. (.2)
2. The consultants discouraged participants by their reactions to the early efforts of the group. (.6)
3. The consultants were not in agreement regarding purposes or ways of working. (.6)
4. The consultants should have made greater use of direct teaching or lecturing. (.8)
5. The change in directors of instruction midway in the project slowed progress. (.8)
6. The consultants did not exercise sufficient initiative. (.8)
7. Some things were done which were not practical—could not be applied. (.8)
8. Differences between junior and senior high school problems tended to destroy unity. (.9)
9. Differences between responsibilities of coordinators and principals made it difficult to get agreement on problems of common concern. (.9)

The responses to three of these items (1, 8, and 9) reflect the feeling that, in general, junior and senior high school principals and coordinators worked harmoniously together hroughout the project. Whatever status differences existed were not troublesome, and the problems faced by the four groups were similar enough to make a unified approach possible.

Four of the items (2, 3, 4, and 6) involved our appraisal of the role played by the consultants from the Institute. Their feeling was that the responses were colored by our genuine desire to maintain good human relations. The consultants themselves were more critical of their role, as has been implied at several points in preceding chapters.

We expected that there would be a substantial inverse correlation between recollection of achievements and recollection of shortcomings. We felt that those who had achieved most, or at least believed they had achieved most, would tend to recall the smallest number of shortcomings. This expectation was not supported by the data. The coefficient of correlation between the two variables was .10.

We also predicted that the people who had expected most from the project might—after the project had been concluded—try to justify the fact that their expectations had not been fulfilled by pointing out that many mistakes had been made. If this prediction had been accurate, we should have obtained a substantial positive correlation between the number of expectations held and the number of shortcomings pointed out. Instead, however, the correlation between expectations and shortcomings was represented by a coefficient of −.19, indicating that there was little relation between the two variables.

Summary

In this chapter we have presented our analyses of evaluation data obtained from a series of inventories administered at the conclusion of the leadership project. Expectations at the beginning of the project, as recalled two and a half years later, were quite diverse, and they varied from one participating group to another. Seventeen major project activities were evaluated, and those who engaged in the greatest number of activities reported that they had benefited most from the project. Many changes in concepts, beliefs, and practices were reported to have taken place. In general, practices were reported to have changed more than beliefs and concepts, although the correlation between changes in these two categories was appreciable. Most of the serious shortcomings of the project were related to lack of time.

APPENDIX

DENVER LEADERSHIP PROJECT PUBLICATIONS

Casey, Veronica, and Corey, Stephen M. "Parents and Teachers Practice Action Research to Cope with Mutual Problems." *Educational Administration and Supervision,* 38:334–341, October 1952.

Corey, Stephen M. "Curriculum Development through Action Research." *Educational Leadership,* 7:147–153, December 1949.

Corey, Stephen M., and Halverson, Paul. "The Educational Leader's Ideas about His Interpersonal Relations." *The Bulletin of the National Association of Secondary-School Principals,* 36:57–63, October 1952.

Corey, Stephen M., Foshay, Arthur W., and Mackenzie, Gordon N. "Instructional Leadership and the Perceptions of the Individuals Involved." *The Bulletin of the National Association of Secondary-School Principals,* 35:83–91, November 1951.

Mackenzie, Gordon N., and Corey, Stephen M. "A Conception of Educational Leadership." *The Bulletin of the National Association of Secondary-School Principals,* 36:9–14, January 1952.

Smith, Mary Neel. "Action Research to Improve Teacher Planning Meetings." *The School Review,* 60:142–150, March 1952.

Smith, Mary Neel. "Making Parent Discussion Groups More Effective." *The School Review,* 60:331–337, September 1952.

"IDEAS ABOUT MYSELF" INVENTORY

Date ....   *Adapted from National*
                                                       Training Laboratory
Name ....   *Form JJJ 50*

The statements below should be responded to in such a way as to give the best possible picture of what you are like. There are no "right" answers. We are all different. Try not to be too critical of or too favorable to yourself. Use the following response key:

⊕   Statement describes me very accurately.
+   Statement is quite descriptive of me.
?   Statement is both true and untrue as a description of me.
—   Statement is generally not a true description of me.
⊖   Statement is decidedly false as a description of me.

1. I think I have a pretty clear understanding of how the people I work with see themselves and the job they are trying to do.
2. I am not the kind of person who can stand up to his superiors and disagree with them.
3. It is important for me to maintain my individuality within any group to which I belong.
4. My relations with other people never present much difficulty for me.
5. I enjoy following a good leader more than being a leader myself.
6. I will stand up for my own ideas even under a lot of pressure from others to change.
7. I often get so involved in doing a particular job that I don't pay

202

much attention to the feelings and reactions of other people concerned.

8. My first reaction to a proposal that things be done differently is usually negative.
9. I try to have things thoroughly thought out before taking an active part in the group.
10. I am aware of most of the shortcomings in my social behavior.
11. I always try to achieve a position of power in a group.
12. I feel I am more fully expressing my personality when I am working in a group than at any other time.
13. I am often tactless and hurt people's feelings without meaning to.
14. I often get so wound up in what I want to say that I do not really listen to what other people are saying.
15. I do not like to express my ideas unless I know they have the support of others.
16. I usually react positively to new people.
17. I am pretty good at taking initiative in a group to keep things moving along.
18. If I believe in something, I will work for it even when this requires opposing friends and associates.
19. I do not pay enough attention to the needs and feelings of individuals with whom I work.
20. I am better at arguing than at conciliating and compromising.
21. I am easily persuaded by others to see things their way.
22. I often detach myself psychologically from the group and just watch what is going on.
23. When someone is talking, I not only listen to what he says but also notice how people react to the things he says.
24. I find it very frustrating to have to work on an important project with other people instead of alone.
25. I get quite upset when people allow their personal feelings to affect the work they are doing.
26. I am quite fearful about going into new social situations.
27. I am happier when working on a project with others than I am when working on something of my own.
28. I can usually predict the reactions of people I know to new suggestions.
29. I enjoy sticking up for my own ideas.
30. I cannot stand up against others in support of unpopular ideas.
31. I am pretty good at finding ways of bringing together two people who seem to be disagreeing.
32. I think I have quite a lot of influence on other people.

33. I sometimes feel that a group or relationship in which I am involved gets so strong that it hampers my individuality and freedom.

34. I am often amazed at the variety of impressions different participants have of the same meeting.

35. It is relatively easy for me to persuade people to see things my way.

36. It does not matter to me whether other people agree with my opinions or not.

37. I get emotionally upset when a group member begins to introduce side issues into the group discussion.

38. I do not like to have the final responsibility for making decisions.

39. I would say I am more likely to dominate a group than to be dominated by it.

40. I am able to silence a group member tactfully when he attempts to introduce his personal feelings into the discussion.

41. I feel blocked and frustrated in my own school situation because of the difficulties resulting from the attitudes of certain people there.

42. I work better with individuals than I do in a group.

43. I feel very much on the spot when people discuss faults I know I have.

44. I take a lot of initiative in starting new activities or procedures.

45. I can make a greater contribution by working as part of a group than I can by working alone.

INDEX

Abilities and needs of teachers, 52–56

Action research, viii, 95, 96, 119 f., 136, 194, 195

Agenda building, cooperative, 145–150

Agenda flexibility, value of, 150 f.

Appointed committees, 141–143

Attitudes and beliefs, 60–62

Bargaining:
  evaluation of, 27 f.
  as leadership method, 16, 22, 24, 27 f.

"Bench marks," 112

Building teams in Denver leadership project:
  difficulties encountered by, 134 f.
  problems studied by, 124–126
  procedures used by, 126–133
  projects of, vii, 108 f., 112, 124–134, 174

Casey, Veronica, ix, 201

Caswell, Hollis L., vi, ix, 103

Central office personnel, 60, 61

Climate, see Psychological climate

Committees:
  appointed and elected, 141–143
  in Denver leadership project, vii, 110, 121 f., 174, 179 f., 188

factors influencing method of forming, 143 f.
  formation of, 139–145
  volunteer, 140 f.
  see also Groups, small working

Communication:
  consequences of poor, 26, 63
  importance of, for mutual goals-means leadership, 36–39, 64, 67
  improvement of, 88 f.; in small working groups, 154, 156–159
  role of face-to-face discussion in, 67
  as situational factor in leadership, 64–68

Conflict, rivalry, and tension, 62–64

Consultants in Denver leadership project, vii, 107, 133 f., 135 f., 174, 196, 197

Control of means:
  defined, 8
  and power, 34 f.
  and leadership, 7, 8, 9
  as situational factor in leadership, 12 f.
  by status leaders, 19, 23, 24, 26, 27, 150
  by teachers, 26, 27

Cooperative agenda building, 145–150

Cooperative determination of goals and means, *see* Mutually acceptable goals and means, determination of

Coordinator of instruction, *see* Curriculum coordinator

Corey, Stephen M., 49, 201

Counseling, *see* Teacher guidance

Criteria for evaluating leadership, 21 f.

Crutchfield, Richard S., 9

Curriculum coordinator:
  instructional responsibility of, 22
  role of, in Denver, 104 f.
  see also Status leader

Darrah, Lucille, ix

Data:
  interpretation of, 96, 130 f.
  sources of, 129 f.

Denver curriculum improvement policy, 105 f.

Denver leadership project:
  building teams, *see* Building teams in Denver leadership project
  committees, vii, 110, 121 f., 174, 179 f., 188
  consultants, vii, 107, 133 f., 135 f., 174, 196, 197
  evaluation of, *see* Evaluation of Denver leadership project
  findings relating to small working groups, 137–167
  groups participating in, listed, vii, 171
  meetings of total group, vii, 90, 107, 109, 112–118, 174
  setting, 103–110
  subgroups, vii, 90, 108, 109, 110, 118–123, 173, 174
  workshop, vii, 109 f., 123, 136, 174
  see also Improvement of leadership

Elected committees, 141 f.

Evaluation of Denver leadership project:
  achievements, 174–179
  expectations, 168–173
  leadership concepts, 187–193

leadership practices, 179–187
learning activities, 173 f.
mistakes, 193–197
see also "Bench marks"

Evaluation of leadership, 26, 27, 28 f., 33–35, 41 f.

Force:
  evaluation of, 26
  as leadership method, 16, 22, 24–27

Formal school organization, 68–70

Foshay, Arthur W., 49, 201

Generalizing, 96, 131–133

Goals:
  assistance in achieving, 6–8, 35, 149 f.
  assistance in identifying, 5 f., 36–38, 87, 90, 147 f.
  compatibility of means and, in leadership education program, 76
  implications of variations in, for selection of leaders, 11
  as situational factors in leadership, 11
  staff members' perceptions of, 37
  of status leaders, 22, 23, 26, 40
  of teachers, 23, 24, 26
  see also Mutually acceptable goals and means, determination of

Goal seeking, relation of leadership to, 4 f.

Gouldner, Alvin W., 9

Group process, 90 f., 108, 123, 157, 174

Groups, informal, 70–73

Groups, small working:
  arrangements for meetings of, 151–156
  improving communication in, 154, 156–159
  increasing participation in, 159–163
  increasing productivity of, 137–167
  leadership in, 137–167
  methods of forming, 137, 139–145
  obstacles to effective work of, 166 f.

task identification by, 145–151
use of forms and records in, 157, 159, 163–166
Guidance, *see* Teacher guidance

Hall, James, ix
Halverson, Paul, 201
Help, giving and receiving of, as key to leadership, 4 f.
Hinderman, Roy, ix
Horace Mann-Lincoln Institute of School Experimentation, vii, 106, 107
Hypothesizing, 91–93, 124–126, 127–129

"Ideas about Myself" inventory, 84 f., 202–204
Improvement of leadership:
  conditions essential to, 76–82
  and control of means, 9
  learning experiences contributing to, 96–100
  learning process involved in, 82–96
Individual differences:
  in abilities and needs, 52–56
  in conception of roles, 47 f.
  in motivation for work, 44–46
  in perception and behavior, 48–52
  as situational factors in leadership, 43–56
Informal school organization, 70–73
In-service education, 53, 54, 75
Instructional leader, *see* Status leader
Interpersonal relations:
  attitudes and beliefs in, 60–62
  and communication, 64–68
  conflict, rivalry, and tension in, 62–64
  and patterns of participation, 58 f.
  and psychological climate, 57 f.
  as situational factors in leadership, 56–68

Keath, Mary Lee, ix
Knickerbocker, Irving R., 9, 120
Krech, David, 9
Leader:
  functions of, 47, 88
  official, *see* Status leader

potential, 9, 13, 74 f.
recognized, 6, 7, 9; defined, 10
selection of, 14–18, 23
unofficial, 72
unrecognized, 6, 7 f.
Leadership:
  as accompaniment of goal seeking, 4 f.
  conditions of, 23
  criteria for evaluating, 21 f.
  evaluation of, 26, 27, 28 f., 33–35, 41 f.
  improvement of, *see* Improvement of leadership
  meaning of, 4–10
  methods, *see* Bargaining, Force, Mutually acceptable goals and means, determination of, and Paternalism
  process, 3, 4 f.
  recognized, 6, 7, 8, 9; defined, 10, 21
  situational factors in, *see* Situational factors in leadership
  traits, 19, 88
  unrecognized, 7, 8
Leadership education program, *see* Improvement of leadership
Leadership learning process, 82–96

Mackenzie, Gordon N., 49, 201
McGregor, Douglas, 9, 57
Means:
  control of, *see* Control of means
  compatibility of goals and, in leadership education program, 76
  exploring and identifying, 7, 9, 29 f., 33, 38 f.
  implications of variations in, for selection of leaders, 11 f., 17 f.
  providing, and leadership, 8, 10, 21, 34, 150
  as situational factors in leadership, 11 f., 15–18
  using and testing, 39 f.
  see also Mutually acceptable goals and means, determination of
Meetings:
  agenda building for, 145–148

evaluation of, *see* Post-meeting evaluation questionnaires

improving communication in, 154, 156–159

increasing participation in, 59, 159–163

opportunities for acquaintance of members, 154–156

physical arrangements for, 152 f.

time allotment for, 153 f.

of total group in Denver leadership project, vii, 90, 107, 109, 112–118, 174

see also Groups, small working

Motivation for work, 44–46

Mutually acceptable goals and means, determination of:

climate necessary for, 30, 35, 36, 40, 45, 145

evaluation of, as leadership method, 33–35, 41 f.

as integrated process, 30

in leadership education program, 76 f.

as leadership method, 17, 22, 24, 29 f.

as relation between individuals, 30

status leader and, 29 f., 35–41, 87, 90, 149 f.

Oberholzer, Kenneth, ix

Official leader, *see* Status leader

Participation in group work:

methods of increasing, 59, 159–163

patterns of, 58 f.

Paternalism:

evaluation of, 28 f.

as leadership method, 16 f., 22, 24, 28 f.

Perception and behavior, 48–52

Permissive atmosphere, 30, 36, 40, 65, 81, 138, 145

Personnel, as situational factors in leadership, 43–73

Personnel services, 52–56

Pfiffner, John M., 43

Post-meeting evaluation questionnaires, 56, 85 f., 90, 94, 95,

116 f., 122, 130, 148 f., 153, 158, 162, 164, 165, 166

Potential leaders, 9, 13, 74 f.

Principals:

instructional responsibility of, 22

role of, in Denver, 103 f.

see also Status leader

Psychological climate:

permissive, *see* Permissive atmosphere

as situational factor in leadership, 14, 18, 31 f., 57 f.

Questionnaires, *see* Post-meeting evaluation questionnaires

Rating, *see* Teacher rating

Recognized leader, 6, 7, 9

defined, 10

Recognized leadership, 6, 7, 8, 9

defined, 10, 21

Records:

use of, in small working groups, 157, 159, 163–166

see also Post-meeting evaluation questionnaires

Released time:

and Denver curriculum improvement policy, 105

as factor in committee formation, 143 f.

and leadership education program, 79

Reports, listening and reacting to, 113 f.

Research design, 112 f.

Role-playing, 86 f., 95, 114–117, 156, 158, 173, 174

Roles, conception of, 47 f.

School organization:

formal, 68–70

informal, 70–73

as situational factor in leadership, 68–73

School system policy, as situational factor in leadership, 31 f.

Security, importance of, 45, 57, 81, 85

see also Permissive atmosphere

Selection of leaders, 14–18, 23

tuational factors in leadership:
communication, 64–68
control of means, 12 f.
goals, 11
individual differences, 43–56
interpersonal relations, 56–68
means, 11 f.
personnel, 43–73
physical conditions, 14
psychological climate, 14, 18, 31 f., 57 f.
school organization, 68–73
school system policy, 31 f.
mall groups, *see* Groups, small working
mith, Mary Neel, ix, 201
tatus leader:
and bargaining, 27 f.
defined, 3
and determination of mutually acceptable goals and means, 29 f., 35–41, 87, 90, 149 f.
factors influencing selection of leadership method by, 31 f.
and force, 24–27
goals of, 22, 23, 26, 40
instructional responsibility of, 22
and paternalism, 28 f.
responsibility of, for personnel services, 53–56

Subgroups in Denver leadership project, vii, 90, 108, 109, 110, 118–123, 173, 174

Task identification:
and cooperative agenda building, 145–150
and agenda flexibility, 150 f.
Teacher guidance, 54, 55 f.
Teacher rating, 53 f., 143
Teacher transfer, 54
Teams, *see* Building teams in Denver leadership project
Transfer, *see* Teacher transfer

Unofficial leader, 72
Unrecognized leader, 6, 7 f.
Unrecognized leadership, 7, 8

Volunteer committees, 140 f.

Wagner, Ruth, ix
Ways of exercising leadership, *see* Bargaining, Force, Mutually acceptable goals and means, determination of, and Paternalism
Workshop in Denver leadership project, vii, 109 f., 123, 136, 174